A Permanent Crisis

Marc Chesney

A Permanent Crisis

The Financial Oligarchy's Seizing of Power and the Failure of Democracy

Marc Chesney
Department of Banking and Finance
University of Zurich
Zürich, Switzerland

ISBN 978-3-030-00517-7   ISBN 978-3-030-00518-4   (eBook)
https://doi.org/10.1007/978-3-030-00518-4

Library of Congress Control Number: 2018954556

Cover credit: incamerastock/Alamy Stock Photo/Fatima Jamadar

This Palgrave Macmillan imprint is published by the registered company Springer Nature Switzerland AG
The registered company address is: Gewerbestrasse 11, 6330 Cham, Switzerland

To my family and those dear to me.
In memory of my parents.

Preface

The title of this book may be surprising. It might even seem contradictory to evoke a "permanent crisis" when, at the same time as this book is going to print, the media are talking about a resurgence in economic growth and, according to so-called experts, economic fundamentals are healthy, even strong. Proof of this would lie in rising stock markets. Even the February 2018 financial crash has already been forgotten and is now considered to be no more than a "simple correction".

Strangely enough, until today, none of these commentators has mentioned the artificiality of this growth which is essentially based on the explosion in global debt, or the increasing disconnection between bullish stock markets and the performance of both companies and the overall economy. Nor, for that matter, have they alluded to the astronomical sums perpetually injected into the financial sector by central banks in order to keep the too big to fail banks afloat, or to every sort of advantage from which they have benefited, most often at citizens' expense.

For many economic commentators, enhanced labour statistics also appear to constitute one of these encouraging "fundamentals". It seems anecdotal therefore that numerous unemployed have disappeared from the statistics and reappeared as working poor or impoverished pensioners. Whereas the emergence of new technologies and the expansion of digitalisation of the economy should result in more leisure time, the main consequence until now has been an increase in casual employment and under-employment.

Regarding the trickle-down theory often put forward by the media, it does not seem to obey the law of gravity, seeing that, in this case, it works from the bottom-up, and allows those who are already the wealthiest in the world, to accumulate even more wealth.

The operation was a success, they lead us to believe, but the patient, in this case society, is still ill. It is precisely on this skilful trickery presented as an effective economic remedy that these positive "fundamentals" lie.

This book endeavours to provide an objective assessment of reality which is quite different. It describes the currently operative financialisation of the economy and of society and the role of the big banks and hedge funds in this process. It denounces financial croupiers' state of mind and the mercenaries of the financial war, the consequences of which affect each of us every day and in every corner of the world.

Zürich, Switzerland   Marc Chesney

Acknowledgements

The author would like to thank the University of Zurich for the academic freedom granted to him. Furthermore, he would like to express his particular gratitude to his colleagues and friends Paul Dembinski, Paul Embrechts and Jean-Charles Rochet for their enlightening comments and support. He would also like to express his gratitude to Alexandre Shargorodsky for the fruitful exchanges at various times throughout the writing of this book in both its English, French and German versions. He would also like to thank Michael Dornan for his translation from French into English, Kristin Fuchs for her meticulous revision as well as Katharina Serafimova, Carlos Vargas and Isabelle Zheng for their valuable comments.

Finally, his deepest gratitude goes to his parents. Their personality, courage and culture have always guided his pen. It is from the bottom of his heart that he dedicates this book to their memory.

Every year, the Consul General of Switzerland in Frankfurt selects a recently published work and invites its author to present it at the Frankfurt Book Fair. In 2014, his choice was the German version of this book.

Contents

Contents

Introduction: The Sinking of Civilisation in the Name of Its Salvation

Saturday evening, 1 August 1914, French and German families are preparing themselves for the heartbreak of separation. Orders for a general mobilisation have just been posted. The town and village church bells ring endlessly. They bear the dreaded news of the declaration of war, already echoing the fears and suffering to come. The first day of mobilisation will be Sunday, 2 August. From the crack of dawn, Paris's Gare de l'Est is packed full of soldiers accompanied by their families. The scenario is identical at Berlin's Anhalter station. In the name of civilisation's salvation, they will be both the players and the victims of its destruction.

Friday, 1 August 2014, 100 years later, a great number of French and German families are getting ready for their holidays. The next day, the high-speed trains, the TGV at the Gare de Lyon in Paris or the ICE at Central Station in Berlin will be packed full of people. In France, the so-called *autoroute du soleil*, the main motorway linking northern France with the Mediterranean Sea, is congested with its usual traffic jams. The crowds now flock to the south with its beaches instead of the western or eastern front one century ago. The nightmare of a long World War has now been transformed into the dream of sun and sea. It is no longer a question of saving civilisation, but more prosaically of a healthy break while financial and economic instability lingers on. In the height of summer in the centre of Europe, it is the business of tourism that now reigns and helps draw people's attention away from the imbalances that casino finance generates, momentarily relieving the tension associated with it. The mass graves of the First World War are now being eroded from our collective memory.

The monumental painting at the Gare de l'Est in Paris recalls those dreadful events of the First World War. Can it be compared to the wall paintings of the Lascaux caves,[1] to the traces of a remote past, the influences of which have been lost over time?

---

[1]The Lascaux caves, located in Dordogne, is one of the most important sites of prehistoric parietal art.

Abstract

How can we understand the current state of affairs, anticipate and forge a future for society without analysing its history and, in particular, the critical periods of wars and crises that have preceded us? Reflecting upon the First World War provides us with a wealth of knowledge. A century has elapsed since the sacrifice of European youth—in particular French, German and English—in the mass graves of the Great War. Today, in the heart of Europe, the trenches have fortunately disappeared but current generations suffer from a profound crisis with financial and economic ramifications. These, along with other social, environmental and political issues are addressed in this book.

At that time, the majority of the population did not believe that a war would break out, or if it was the case, they could not conceive anything other than a brief one. It did, however, and it lasted four long years.

Nowadays, worldwide, despite numerous government statements regarding financial imbalances, the system continues to fail at an accelerating pace and the casual labour phenomenon is evolving. This book analyses the whys of this situation and draws parallels between the society of 1914 and that of today while providing a number of solutions to casino finance.

1

Yesterday and Today

A century has already elapsed since the sacrifice of Europe's youth in the mass graves of the First World War. One hundred years seems a lot, and yet it only covers a few generations and a society, that of 1914, very close to our own, with its universities, its libraries, its operas, its theatres and literature, with its parliament, its law courts, and of course its businesses and its banks. The West could then boast of its economic, social and scientific, as well as democratic, achievements.

Of course, the Internet was a long way away but radio had already been invented and print media were already well developed and probably more diversified and less regulated than they are today. Commercial flights were not yet in existence but it was already possible to travel by train and car.

An educated, civilised society in which two countries, France and Germany, at the height of their influence, both of Christian tradition, sharing the same fundamental principles, engage in a disastrous war with weapons of mass destruction of the time. The assassination of the archduke Franz Ferdinand, crown prince and heir to the Austro-Hungarian Empire in Sarajevo on 28 June 1914 is the spark that ignites Europe and enfolds it in a spiral of destruction, the sacrifice of

© The Author(s) 2018
M. Chesney, *A Permanent Crisis*,
https://doi.org/10.1007/978-3-030-00518-4_1

a whole generation, and the material and moral ruin of its civilisation in its name. The wide-scale manipulation of the crowds is the process by which they are caught up in this barbarity in the name of safeguarding democracy or the nation. This is evidenced in a major work of the time, *The Thibaults*, in which its author, Roger Martin du Gard, speaks through its hero with the following words: "Never has humanity experienced such a spell, such blindness of intelligence!"[1] In *All Quiet on the Western Front*, author Erich Maria Remarque also reveals this descent of humanity as the central character of his novel, a German soldier, claims:

> We are burnt up by hard facts; like tradesmen we understand distinctions, and like butchers, necessities. ...we are terribly indifferent... we are crude and sad and superficial—I believe we are lost.[2]

They were lost in the trenches, in a horrible and senseless battle. Aren't we also lost today? The indifference, the crudeness, the sadness and the superficiality might also characterise our generations, especially the mercenaries of the financial war.

The Trader, a Twenty-First-Century Mercenary

The following text message exchange between two present-day young mercenaries is an instructive example of this:

– hi
– hi
– it's death
– david from CS called about *skew trades* (...)
– I'm telling you, they'll smash us to pieces (...), tonight you'll have at least 600M

---

[1]Personal translation from: Martin du Gard, Roger, Les Thibault, éd. *Bibliothèque de la pléiade*, Paris, Gallimard, 1955, vol. II, p. 698.
[2]Remarque, Erich Maria, *All Quiet on the Western Front*, Glencoe/McGraw-Hill, USA, 2000, p. 55.

What can this warlike and simplistic, even trivial jargon possibly mean between two supposedly educated individuals? Is he referring to the notion of death? It is not 600 murders because here death is financial. The 600M refers to $600 million in losses which would eventually reach $6 billion. Are *skew trades* weapons of mass destruction? Unfortunately, these financial bets based on complex financial derivative products resemble them all too well.

On 23 March 2012, in JP Morgan's London trading room, trader Bruno Iksil, known as the "London Whale" because of his outsized financial bets, and his assistant Julien Grout realised that their gigantic bets were losing gamble. Their text messages express their despair. Only a year earlier in 2011, Mr. Iksil had successfully bet on the collapse of several American companies. Those bets brought in profits of $400 million for JP Morgan, $32 million of which were in fees for Mr. Iksil and two of his hierarchical superiors.

An additional piece of evidence gives us a more precise description of the frame of mind that exists in investment banks. The author is Fabrice Tourre, the *École Centrale Paris* undergraduate and Stanford graduate who was hired by Goldman Sachs at the age of 22. Some of his emails were used by the Securities and Exchange Commission (SEC) which accused this investment bank of taking advantage of its clients, i.e. the bank incited them to buy very dubious mortgage-backed debt securities while at the same time betting on these securities to plummet. Here is an example of his prose:

> There is more and more leverage in the system. The whole building may collapse at any time. [...] When I think there was a little of me in the creation of this product [...], the kind of thing you invent saying to yourself: what about creating a machine that serves no purpose at all, that is totally conceptual and highly theoretical and that nobody knows how to price, it is bad for the heart to watch it implode in full flight. It is a little like Frankenstein turning against his inventor.[3]

---

[3]See: Warde Ibrahim, «Des Français qui gagnent», *Le Monde Diplomatique*, July 2010, own translation.

An email written by another young man confirms this same state of despair. Jérôme Kerviel, the trader who generated a loss of $4.9 billion for Société Générale in 2007, wrote the following email. "In a trading room, the ideal modus operandi can be summed up in one phrase: knowing how to take the maximum risk to gain the bank the maximum money. In the name of such rule, the most elementary principles of caution don't count for much."... "In the midst of the great banking orgy, traders have the same consideration as any average prostitute: the quick acknowledgment that today's paycheck was good".[4] Since then, he has been convicted whereas his employer was let off scot-free, despite a certain responsibility in spreading the casino economy and the disastrous mentality associated with it.

Finally, Sam Polk, a former trader, brought to light another dimension of the problem. For him, as for a number of his colleagues, money became a drug. Here is an extract from his prose:

> Not only was I not helping to fix any of the world's problems but I was profiting from them. In my last year on Wall Street my bonus was $3.6 million — and I was angry because it wasn't big enough. I was 30 years old, had no children to raise, no debts to pay, no philanthropic goal in mind. I wanted more money for exactly the same reason an alcoholic needs another drink: I was addicted.[5]

When reading these emails and testimonials, other features from today's society emerge. Within this financial sphere, the central nervous system of the economy, venality or the almost total absence of non-financial values as well as a moral void dominate. The raw cynicism of young disillusioned men or women, addicted to money, fresh out of the best academic institutions, is not only tolerated but almost implicitly encouraged by their employers. At this stage, it should be pointed out that these institutions often take pride in training such brilliant subjects, capable of operating in the trading rooms of the biggest

[4]Ibid and Rogue trader Jérôme Kerviel's trial begins in Paris, *The Guardian*, 6 July 2010.
[5]Folk Sam, "For the Love of Money", *The New York Times*, Sunday Review, online, 18 January 2014.

international banks. Universities usually do not encourage and prepare their students to question the social usefulness of the financial sector's functioning and to reflect with a critical spirit on the realism of mainstream economic assumptions and models. The large-scale hiring of traders, too often selected and trained to behave like soulless mercenaries, helps these banks to be an active part in today's financial war where the stakes of the casino economy[6] become weapons of mass destruction[7] that shake countries, companies and society at large.

Another characteristic deserves mention. A large part of today's society is *disoriented*, as it is faced with a distressful situation in which there appears to be no way out.

A War Without Borders

Today, the youth of Europe no longer dies *en masse* in the trenches or on battlefields. Those who do die early owe it rather to road accidents or suicides.[8] They are enlisted in this other form of war that is the financial war from which it most often suffers. Depression,[9] alcoholism[10] and obesity are its ills, and these are the side effects of distress. Its fears: the future and the risks of unemployment and insecurity generated by financial instability. The media confuses today's generations by very often displaying as essential what is actually futile, and only addressing the essential in the most futile of manners at best. As they do not have the keys to understand what is truly at stake, the future appears

---

[6]On this topic, the following book is a reference: Sinn, Hans-Werner, *Casino Capitalism*, Oxford University Press, 2012.

[7]In 2003, investor Warren Buffet declared that derivatives are "weapons of mass destruction".

[8]According to the World Health Organisation, all over the world close to 1.25 million people die from road accidents every year, 800,000 people commit suicide, that it to say one every 40 seconds, and at least 20 times more attempt it. See: *Global Status Report on Road Safety*, WHO, 2015 and *Suicide Data: A Global Imperative*, WHO, 2015.

[9]According to the World Health Organisation, more than 300 million people suffer from depression. See the report: *Mental Health*, WHO, April 2017.

[10]According to the World Health Organisation, all over the world close to 3.3 million people die from alcoholism.

too often as indecipherable and therefore unsettling. Mass underemployment[11] has been permanently installed in our society resulting in an increase in job insecurity and a marginalisation of whole chunks of the population. For someone who is unemployed, being excluded from the world of employment means it is impossible to build a life or new horizons. The warlike vocabulary demonstrates the scale of the destructiveness. Over the course of 100 years has the "battle for jobs" become a new "battle of the Marne"? Probably not, if on the French side the battle of the Marne was a victory, the outcome of the "battle for employment" remains very hazy and there are no winners. The resurgence in economic growth will not lead to economic stabilisation and the massive creation of sustainable jobs.

More generally, all over the world, the financial crisis generated around 30 million unemployed,[12] without counting all those who are not included in the official statistics. Increases in labour productivity within the current context of limited growth often have the effect of increasing unemployment instead of creating more free time, as it should be the case in a well-organised society.

This crisis seems to have taken on a permanent nature because the measures taken to supposedly correct financial imbalances do little but extend it. In fact, it is profound and is the result of a global financial war that robs and causes large-scale impoverishment of a large majority of the world's population. The financial Moloch requires sacrifices. This conflict is very one-sided, as it is essentially being waged by a financial plutocracy, a tiny minority that represents only around 0.01% of the global population.

The theatres of this war are many and are situated on different continents. Europe is one of them, with Greece as its special focal point. Some neighbourhoods in Athens have been devastated by this conflict

---

[11]According to the European Central Bank (ECB), "extended unemployment", which includes underemployment, affects 15% of the active population of the Eurozone and is therefore much higher than the official unemployment rate of 9%. See the third section of the ECB's *Economic Bulletin*, dated 10 May 2017.

[12]See the International Labour Organisation (ILO) report entitled: "World Employment and Social Outlook: Trends 2016", dated January 2016.

and by this highly intense financial crisis. Both the regular clashes between demonstrators and police forces until the elections on 25 January 2015 and unemployment and large-scale job insecurity are the traits of this financial and social war undertaken by the European Commission, the European Central Bank (ECB) and the International Monetary Fund (IMF).

Africa is another theatre of this war without borders. Many countries that are the losers of this economic and financial conflict are situated on this continent. One of the consequences of their defeat is to have to put up with more and more industrial pollution from the developed world, i.e. to be used as its dumping ground. We know that the flagship of modernity, the computer sector, produces thousands of tonnes of electronic trash. Certain African countries, Ghana in particular, have become vast open landfills. Children, adolescents, instead of going to school, try day after day with anything they can find to dismantle our broken down computers to extract certain metals and resell them. They are exposed to toxic products. Their work is dangerous. Everyday survival is a permanent battle.

Furthermore, regarding food, unbridled speculation has created a shortage for many Africans.[13] In 2008, for example, according to FAO,[14] over 900 million people suffered from malnutrition. However, world grain production that year would have been more than sufficient to feed the whole population.[15] These days, every 24 hours, some 25,000 people, of whom 8600 are children, die of hunger.[16]

America is also a theatre of this vast war. Large numbers of people suffer from its consequences. Wall Street taps numerous engineers, computer scientists, jurists, physicists and mathematicians that the USA need in other sectors. Subsidies and all types of advantages received by

---

[13]See the books *Mordshunger* by Jean Feyder published by Westend publishers in Germany in 2014 and the one by Jean Ziegler entitled *Destruction Massive*, Seuil, 2011.

[14]Source: FAO, Global hunger declining, but still unacceptably high, 2010.

[15]On this topic, see the book entitled: *Bet the Farm: How Food Stopped Being Food*, de Frederick Kaufman, Wiley, 2012.

[16]Source: FAO, *World Food Situation*, 2017 and Welthungerhilfe, Hunger—Verbreitung Ursachen und Folgen, 2017.

big banks[17] and hedge funds allow them to offer compensations that are out of proportion with those offered elsewhere.

Intellectual resources and public funds wasted in this way are needed in other sectors of activity which are essential to the population. Upgrading the country's infrastructure, such as railways and airports, should therefore be a priority as they meet the needs of the huge majority who do not have helicopters or private jets to travel in. Investing in areas such as health and education ought to be another. Hospitals, schools and public universities manifestly require vast amounts of funds.[18] Repairing bridges and pipelines and guaranteeing the maintenance of dams[19] are responsibilities of a government. Unfortunately, these tasks have seemingly become of secondary importance. The financial sector is calling the shots to ensure that its interests prevail. Between 1998 and 2008, it spent $1.7 billion to fund the electoral campaigns of its allies and $3.4 billion on its lobbying activities.[20] According to *Fortune* magazine,[21] Wall Street spent $2 billion to influence the 2016 US elections. This included contributions for the Presidential, Senate and House of Representatives elections. This investment was cleverly hedged with 55% for the Republicans and 45% for the Democrats and included the Trump and Clinton campaigns. Contributions made by main banks, Wells Fargo, Citibank and Goldman Sachs, were between $12 and $15 million each, JPMorgan Chase, Bank of America and Morgan Stanley $10 million each. The hedge fund Renaissance Technologies spent $53 million!

---

[17]See Chapter 4.

[18]According to the National Education Association, an amount of approximately $322 billion would be required to renovate schools. See: *Third World America*, Arianna Huffington, Crown Publisher, New York, 2009, p. 113.

[19]According to the Department of Transportation, one in every four bridges suffers from structural deficiencies or is dilapidated. On average, they have a lifespan of 50 years and were constructed 43 years ago. According to an analysis by the *New York Times* conducted based on data from the Environmental Agency, a large pipeline explodes on average every two minutes. Ibid., pp. 100 and 106.

[20]Ibid., p. 130, as well as *13 Bankers*, Simon Johnson and James Kwak, Pantheon Books, New York, 2010.

[21]See: "Wall Street Spent $2 Billion Trying to Influence the 2016 Election", *Fortune Magazine*, 8 March 2017.

Wall Street wants to maintain its position in the war against Main Street. The growth of the financial sector is dangerous for the economy and society. From the onset of the 1950s to 2006, this sector has gone from representing 2.8% of GDP to representing 8.3%.[22] This increase has emphasised economic and social imbalances and in 2008 resulted in a crisis that is still dragging on and the chronic disturbances of which affect society both in the USA and in other countries.

At the beginning of 2015 in Brazil, this financial war took on a new meaning. The country was suffering from a lack of liquidity in the primary sense of the term. We are talking about water, essential to life! The southeast of Brazil was suffering from a huge drought. The reserves had reached unprecedented lows. In the emergency and in order to meet requirements, the State of São Paulo considered using a polluted water reservoir as well as open sewers for industry. Two phenomena explain this situation. On the one hand, rainfall is far too low. On the other hand, when it does rain, the water is lost in the sewers. It is likely that the continuous deforestation of the Amazon is the true cause of the former. As to the latter phenomenon, Sabesp, the company responsible for providing São Paulo with water has not proceeded to make any serious investments in the pipelines for a number of years. It prefers to pay out large dividends than to invest in modernising the network. Between 2007 and 2014, the profits of this company, one of the most profitable in the country, totalled close to 10 billion reals, i.e. €3.23 billion. About a third of that sum went to both public and private shareholders. Dividends of such a scale are rare in this sector of activity. What was left over from the profits was not invested responsibly. The rate of water leakage is 36% in São Paulo in 2015, which corresponds to 435 billion litres a year! For this company, investing in the maintenance of the pipelines would reduce short-term profits, whereas letting the water leak only represents a tiny part of costs.[23] Bonuses distributed to its directors are only based on realised profits, with no indicator of efficiency being taken into consideration.

---

[22]See: *The Growth of Finance*, Robin Greenwood and David Scharfstein, 2013.

[23]See the article written by Maria Luíza Filgueiras in the Brazilian magazine *EXAME* and published by EXAME.com on 24 November 2014.

Short-term financial thinking is the cause of these two phenomena. It corresponds to the interest of a so-called elite that is very often corrupt and to the detriment of the basic needs of the population. Short-term profit maximisation is indeed a key characteristic of today's destructive monetary and financial system and is the cause of many environmental and social imbalances.

How We Got to This Point

From 1814 to 1914, i.e. approximately from the end of the Napoleonic wars to the outbreak of the First World War, mankind witnessed a century of social, economic and scientific development, unique in its history. On the contrary, the hundred years that followed were not up to expectations with over two hundred million deaths caused by war and conflict.[24] The First World War followed by the Wall Street Crash of 1929 resulted in the rise of terrifying dictatorships mainly in Germany and the former USSR, but also in Italy, Spain and Japan. The increase in power of these dictators led to the Second World War with its bloodshed and death camps. With the American bombing of Hiroshima and Nagasaki, the end of the Second World War marked mankind's, or rather what was left of it, entry into the nuclear era, military as well as civil, with the clash of two superpowers, the USA and the then USSR, within the framework of the cold war. The reconstruction period, known as the Glorious Thirty in France and the German Economic Miracle, would bring about a certain stability and prosperity in Western Europe.

The 1970s marked a turning point with the Vietnam War and the oil crises. With the election of Ronald Reagan in the USA and Margaret Thatcher in Great Britain, the implementation of a neoliberal[25]

---

[24]These are 231 million deaths in the twentieth century. Cf. the book by Milton Leitenberg, entitled: *Deaths in Wars and Conflicts in the 20th Century*, Cornell University, Peace Studies Program, 2006.

[25]Read the excellent book on this topic *Masters of the Universe, Hayek, Friedman, and the Birth of Neoliberal Politics* by Daniel Stedman Jones, Princeton University Press, 2012.

economic policy began first in those two countries followed by most other Western nations. The fall of the Berlin Wall would allow for this policy to be exported to the former USSR and to its former satellite countries. It would also be adopted by China, meaning that today it pervades the entire international scene. According to the American intellectual Francis Fukuyama, the worldwide establishment of the neo-liberal agenda should result in the end of history, an era where not only liberal principles but also their democratic counterparts would allow for balance and peace to prevail in the world. According to him, with the end of the cold war, there would be a global consensus formed around the so-called liberal democracy.

The Manipulation and Control of Public Opinion

Society's current state, based on a financialisation of economic activities, is often presented as the ultimate and therefore unsurpassable phase in the development of capitalism. Well, is it? Is the current situation characteristic of capitalism in full expansion, the outcome of which would be to perpetually dispense its benefits, including its democratic ones, to the whole world? There are grounds for doubt! Doesn't the present situation rather recall that which prevailed in the early twentieth century, when Western civilisation was convinced of its supremacy over the rest of the world, up to the moment when… the First World War broke out? At a time when a new cold war is being organised in Europe, based on or under the pretext of the events in Ukraine, the fall, the accelerated decline of civilisation is already underway. Basic democratic principles are being violated by the PRISM electronic and telephone surveillance programme, as revealed by Edward Snowden.[26] A democratic State should not read its citizen's correspondence, or that of the global population, or spy on people or keep close watch on what they are doing, and tomorrow, technology permitting, try and read their thoughts. It is useful at this point to recall Article 12 of the Universal

---

[26]See: *No Place to Hide* by Glenn Greenwald, Metropolitan Books, New York, 2014.

Declaration of Human Rights: "No one shall be subjected to arbitrary interference with his privacy, family, home or correspondence". The society described by George Orwell in *1984* appears to have become a reality before our very eyes, maybe even surpassed by reality. Technology has allowed nightmares to become a reality! Democracy is crumbling under the intensive and generalised control of the population. Mankind deserves a different type of ending to its own history.

The manipulation of public opinion thanks to the work of fear is at work. Today, it is the financial monsters, presented as national champions that must be rescued from the fear of a cataclysm. Those who issue toxic financial products and benefit from a crisis that they are largely responsible for have to be bailed out with public funds for the sake of stability and economic prosperity! Yesterday, it was on behalf of civilisation, the nation, democracy, a fear of barbarianism and "to put an end to all wars" that one had to wage the so-called last one. In fact, arms manufacturers—Krupp in Germany and Schneider in France—had powerful interests to defend. The fear of colossal financial losses for American banks having lent funds to England and France was one of the essential factors explaining the reasons why the USA joined the war in 1917.

Today like yesterday, in order to cover powerful banks against the risks they took, and to keep them afloat, all sacrifices are being portrayed as necessary, including that of democracy. The following extract from the previously quoted *The Thibaults* is as topical as ever: "Never have the forces of power imposed on people such a total abdication of responsibility…".[27]

Power and Lobbies of the Financial Oligarchy

Thus, democratic principles have today been scorned particularly in the economic field. Indeed, most often, regardless of electoral results, one single policy prevails, that of the financial oligarchy. The latter is so

---

[27]Martin du Gard, Roger, *Les Thibault*, op.cit., p. 698, own translation.

convinced of its superiority and the primacy of its interests over those of the economy and society, presented by its lobbies as a concomitance of interest, that it doesn't even bother discussing them. But that is not the worst. Most politicians are also convinced of it or at least they pretend they are.

This financial caste absorbs astronomical amounts that it is incapable of actually investing in the economy. These amounts always move more quickly within the framework of a casino finance contrary to an entrepreneurial logic which this oligarchy claims, where dubious betting on the bankruptcy of companies, banks or countries takes precedence over standard financial operations inherent to the economy. What characterises these bets is that they are most often made discarding the risks to the rest of society. For those institutions known as "too big to fail", having reached such a critical size and such density of connections within the economic and financial network, it is in fact the State, and at the end of the day the taxpayer, the pensioner, the customer and the unemployed who assumes the risks and, if need be, pays the bills. This financialised economy at such a scale weakens both the economic and social fabric.

So what do political leaders do to remedy this situation and fight against this casino finance? They meet… and what's more, often! And we are supposed to be reassured. Their successive meetings border on the ridiculous and often do little to solve fundamental problems. The performance that the European leaders give is nevertheless well coordinated: red carpet like at the Cannes Festival, public statements followed by talks, then a family photograph, press conference and self-congratulations. It is particularly appalling. The Austrian writer Karl Kraus in his introduction to the *Last Days of Mankind,* a book written with reference to the First World War, alludes to "these years during which the operetta performers performed the tragedy of mankind".[28] A century later, this phrase continues to ring true. These characters, supposedly standing for state authority, often look bewildered. They give the impression they are playing it by ear, with no true sense of direction. Nevertheless, they do

---

[28]Kraus Karl, *The Last Days of Mankind*, Yale University Press, USA, 2015, preface.

have an objective that consists in reassuring the financial markets, which they only manage to achieve temporarily. Their solutions are transient for their objective is in vain. This new religion, neoliberalism, requires sacrifices on the altar of casino finance. Endeavouring to satisfy financial markets is dangerous and illusory.

Bibliography

ECB's *Economic Bulletin*, 10 May 2017.

Feyder, Jean, *Mordshunger*, Westend Publishers, 2014.

Global Status Report on Road Safety, WHO, 2015.

Greenwald, Glenn, *No Place to Hide*, Metropolitan Books, New York, 2014.

Huffington, Arianna, *Third World America*, Crown Publisher, New York, 2009.

International Labour Organisation (ILO) Report: "World Employment and Social Outlook: Trends 2016", January 2016.

Kaufman, Frederick, *Bet the Farm: How Food Stopped Being Food*, Wiley, 2012.

Johnson, Simon, and Kwak, James, *13 Bankers*, Pantheon Books, New York, 2010.

Leitenberg, Milton, *Deaths in Wars and Conflicts in the 20th Century*, Cornell University, Peace Studies Program, 2006.

Martin du Gard, Roger, Les Thibault, éd. *Bibliothèque de la pléiade*, Paris, Gallimard, 1955.

Mental Health, WHO, April 2017.

Remarque, Erich Maria, *All Quiet on the Western Front*, Glencoe/McGraw-Hill, USA, 2000.

Sinn, Hans-Werner, *Casino Capitalism*, Oxford University Press, 2012.

Stedman Jones, Daniel, *Masters of the Universe, Hayek, Friedman, and the Birth of Neoliberal Politics*, Princeton University Press, 2012.

Ziegler, Jean, *Destruction Massive*, Seuil, 2011.

2

Trying to Satisfy Financial Markets Is but a Vain Task

In the work of the Austrian writer Robert Musil, *The Man Without Qualities*,[1] the main characters, before 1914, are planning to organise the commemoration of the 70th anniversary of the accession of the "Emperor of Peace" to be held in Vienna in 1918. What happened? War broke out, Emperor Franz Joseph died in 1916, and the Austro-Hungarian Empire disappeared in 1918. A century later, it is financial markets and their convulsions that plunge the economy and society into dangerous dynamics. Trying to appease them is as vain as wanting, on the eve of the First World War, to celebrate an emperor of peace. In fact, markets are by nature unsatisfied and continually impose new sacrifices.

At the time of the First World War, nations, placed on a pedestal, demanded sacrifices. The supreme sacrifice that consisted of "being killed on the battle field for your homeland" was the lot of millions of Europeans. Today, deified financial markets, demand to be perpetually

---

This chapter is partly taken from my article, Trying to appease financial markets is but a vain and dangerous task, Médiapart, 27 December 2011.

---

[1]Musil, Robert, *The Man Without Qualities*, Vintage, USA, 1996.

© The Author(s) 2018
M. Chesney, *A Permanent Crisis*,
https://doi.org/10.1007/978-3-030-00518-4_2

satisfied, which entails numerous sacrifices for society and the environment. The question of knowing whether such an objective is desirable seems out of place as the answer appears obvious! Of course, if not we could expect the worst: rocketing insolvency of states, downgrades of their rating by rating agencies, all of this resulting in even more drastic austerity programmes. It is nevertheless this type of policy that governments, central banks and international institutions like the IMF most often impose. They all agree. The matter therefore appears to be settled. It would probably be out of place to ask the question about the effectiveness of this policy and its justifications. But let's dare to do so nevertheless.

Devastating Effects of the Crisis

We have no choice but to admit that since the outbreak of the crisis in 2008, this strategy has not really been crowned with success. The south of Europe is more often bled dry, suffering from brutal austerity programmes. In Greece, the government formed on 25 January 2015 has, up to the time this book was written, never known how to, nor been able to reverse this policy. In the third quarter of 2017, the unemployment rate was 20.7%. According to a report from the Greek central bank published in June 2016, 427,000 Greeks between the ages of 15 and 64 had left the Greek republic since 2008. Most of them were young graduates. During the same quarter of 2017, the youth unemployment rate was 40.8%. In terms of comparison, it was 37.9% in Spain and 18.2% in the European Union. Again in Greece, wages had dropped by 24% between 2010 and 2015 and around a third of its inhabitants were living below the poverty line in 2016. Between 2008 and 2012, direct and indirect taxes increased on average by 53 and 22%, respectively. The poorest half of the population saw a much more dramatic increase in taxes: 337%. The standard VAT rate reached completely disproportionate levels and is now at 24% including restaurants![2]

---

[2]Source: A study from the Hans Böckler Foundation, Berlin, 2015.

In 2014, more and more companies, both public and private, no longer paid their workers or suppliers in full. The education budget is also a victim to this policy. Its drastic reduction led to the closing or the clustering of around one thousand schools.

In 2017, Germany, whose economy is often quoted as an example, had around 13 million individuals living below the poverty line, which means close to 16% of its total population. Around 220,000 people, who in this country have "mini jobs" and are paid between 1 and 2 euros an hour, are part of that population and are not considered as unemployed. The low-wage sectors corresponding in 2017 to an hourly wage rate of below €10.50 an hour have seen a strong development in that country. They included at least 7.65 million people at the beginning of that same year, or in other words, 24.3% of the wage-earning population. In Germany, the economic driver of Europe, millions of people survive on miserable wages. The country's improved labour statistics are based on a transformation process from unemployed to working poor.

In 2016 in France, approximately 14% of the population was below the poverty line. 87% of recruitments were made under the form of short-term contracts, which are themselves insecure by nature.

According to UNICEF, in its 2015 alternative report, in France 20% of children, meaning over 3 million of them, found themselves below the poverty line, around 30,000 of them are homeless, up to 8000–10,000 children live in slums or in poor conditions, and every year, close to 140,000 youths under the age of 25 drop out of the school system with no qualifications at all.

In 2016 in Italy, 7.9% of the population were in a situation of extreme poverty, meaning with no possibility of procuring first necessity products and decent housing. In Spain, the drama of evictions continues. They affect families that cannot afford to pay their mortgages and not even the interest on them. According to the Spanish central bank, during the first half of 2016, around 36,000 families had to give up their homes.

In Europe, despite pre-electoral declarations, both left and right wing governments have increased the tax burden on the middle classes and the more disadvantaged members of society. In the USA, the situation is similar to, in 2016, close to 43 million Americans, i.e. 12.7% of the population living below the poverty line. Many of them are excluded from employment statistics because, for example, the unemployed who do not have the right to benefits or those who work at least one hour per month disappear from the statistics. This allowed for the official unemployment rate to be set at 4.1% in March 2018, when in fact it was much higher. The growth that the country underwent in the fourth quarter of 2017 is due in part to the export of arms. From one century to another, the business of fear remains lucrative.

Finally in Japan in 2014, 16% of the population lived below the poverty line.

Trying to satisfy financial markets means bailing out the banking system at the taxpayers' expense, without demanding anything in return. This has led to record indebtedness in developed countries.

"Between October 2008 and October 2011, the European Commission approved €4.5 trillion (equivalent to 37% of EU GDP) of state aid measures to financial institutions".[3] Between 2008 and 2016, the European Commission approved a total of around €5.045 trillion in State aid in favour of the financial sector.

The Ambiguous Role of Central Banks

Central banks by way of their mass intervention have helped prevent the brutal collapse of the banking system during the most critical periods of the crisis. However, by supporting the financial system, they play an essential role within the framework of a financial policy serving the major banks, which does not solve the fundamental problems facing the economy and analysed in this book.

In July 2012, statements made by the then European Central Bank President Mario Draghi, aimed at reassuring the financial markets and according to which this institution was "ready to do whatever it takes to preserve the euro", had the desired effect. Letting it be understood that

---

[3]See the Press Release issued by the European Commission, Michael Barnier, Brussels, 6 June 2012.

the sovereign debt buyback programme, from which Greece, Ireland and Portugal among others benefitted, could be limitlessly reactivated, resulted in a drop in the interest rates on Spanish and Italian debts in particular. But markets are never reassured for long. The ECB was forced to drop its key interest rate to 0.5% in 2013 and to almost zero in 2015.

On 22 January 2015, the President of the ECB announced the establishment of a huge programme to purchase assets of €60 billion, which in April 2016 was increased to €80 billion a month[4] and back to the initial amount in April 2017. Until December 2017,[5] the total amount thus injected in the banking system will have already been higher than €2.3 trillion! Their size should have ensured that these injections were of an urgent nature and therefore limited in time. Yet, they have continued and have brought with them a number of risks.

The future will tell whether the interventions of this European institution will accomplish in a sustainable manner the objective announced: relaunching the economy. In fact, the European Central Bank is in a dead end street. Instead of turning around and changing its policy, it confirms the latter with astronomical resources. By presenting itself as independent of political power, it takes measures favourable to the financial sector.

Furthermore, the ECB grants loans to European banks at very low rates. To benefit from this, they must provide collateral. The ECB is complaisant because it often accepts assets, the quality of which is uncertain,[6] for example, financial securities backed by subprime mortgages from the banks involved with clients whose solvability is dubious. In principle, this lax attitude of the ECB allows these banks to be more lenient as regards mortgage lending conditions to their clients and to receive attractive margins. Indeed, they might lend to this type of clients

---

[4]The assets concerned also include the bonds issued by the States of the Eurozone and by large multinationals, but the latter usually have no concerns about refinancing. Smaller companies however don't really benefit from this ECB programme. This policy will not let them relaunch their investments. See: Die EZB verdrängt private Investoren, *NZZ*, 19 July 2016.

[5]As of January 2018, it is €30 billion per month.

[6]The reference to this subject is the book by Kjell G. Nyborg, entitled: *Collateral Frameworks: The Open Secret of Central Banks*, Cambridge University Press, 2017.

at relatively high rates and borrow from the ECB at low rates. The policy of complacency is risky for the ECB and results in an increased circulation of dubious financial products which the banks get rid of and thus increase the systemic risk.

Being indebted vis-à-vis the ECB at almost zero interest rate also allows them to invest in bonds of certain States in the Eurozone, supposedly at no risk and which have a higher return. This is particularly profitable.[7] With the borrowed funds, these banks proceed to financial arbitrages.[8]

The amounts poured into the financial system on such a large scale by the ECB are not really invested in the economy. The priorities of the big banks are clearly elsewhere. Instead of focusing on what is supposed to be their main activity, i.e. lending capital to European companies with profitable and sustainable investment projects, they are involved in short-term income-generating activities such as financial arbitrages and the dissemination of complex and very often toxic financial products.[9]

Once this liquidity has entered the financial sector, it generates high market returns, in contrast to the economic situation which is not rosy. They contribute to the growing disconnection between the financial and economic sectors, the former thereby hindering economic and social development. The ECB's monetary policy does not essentially improve the resilience of the financial system, which is inherently instable.

In the USA, the purchase of government bonds by the central bank, the FED, led to a considerable increase in its balance sheet, which had already reached approximately $4.5 trillion in July 2017. A smaller amount, but nevertheless enormous, was held central banks, including

---

[7]And especially as this purchase of bonds does not require the possession of supplementary equity. It is as if, for example, the default risk of Greece were non-existent.

[8]Financial arbitrage: Here, it is a case of making an allegedly sure profit without seed money.

[9]Toxic financial products: due to their complexity, these products entail a risk that, at the time of purchase, is not generally perceived by the buyers, i.e. by the unfortunate customer of banks that issue them. When they are sold on a large scale, they generate substantial profit for these banks and a systemic risk for the economy, in the sense that when the toxicity materialises, the customers, companies and individuals will suffer serious financial difficulties. Examples are given in Chapters 3 and 4. Also see the scientific article: Toxic Sustainable Companies? A Critique on the Shortcomings of Current Corporate Sustainability Ratings and a Definition of 'Financial Toxicity', Peter Seele and Marc Chesney, *Journal of Sustainable Finance & Investment*, 2017.

those of Japan, China, Saudi Arabia, with the remainder having been acquired by institutional investors, such as pension funds. In the USA, the injection of funds by the central bank was also carried out on a huge scale and this policy was momentarily stopped. It is indeed a problem to have the FED balance sheet swollen indefinitely to such an extent. In a certain way, US companies are ensuring the follow-through as they continue to inject huge amounts into capital markets. According to Citi analysts,[10] US companies bought back almost $3 trillion of their own shares between 2010 and 2016. Corporate buybacks are expected to reach around $1000 billion in 2018.

In accordance with corporate logic, these colossal amounts should have been used for productive investments, which would have created jobs. Instead, they contributed to the growing disconnection between the financial and economic spheres, as referred to above. They have in fact allowed the stock markets to make a good impression, in contrast to the socio-economic situation. As a result, the CEOs concerned have been more than comfortably compensated, given that bonuses are often based on company stock prices.

In Japan, the central bank's purchases of government bonds are also colossal. In 2014, they represented an amount of close to €600 billion. Such volumes dried up the Japanese debt market. Currently, it holds at least 40% of the total stock of the country's bonds[11] and should hold 50% in 2018.

This institution also purchases vast amounts of stock.[12] In 2016, it was already the main shareholder of the largest 55 companies in the country, namely of those that comprise the Nikkei 225 Index.[13] The results of this monetary policy led to economic growth in 2017. However, the situation remains fragile, due to Japan's enormous public and private debt, and to the deflationary risk which still cannot be ruled out.

---

[10]See: Buyback Outlook Darkens for US Stocks, *Financial Times*, 21 June 2017.

[11]See: Bank of Japan's Expansion of Bond Holdings to Slow in 2018, *Japantimes*, 18 December 2017.

[12]The National Swiss Bank is no exception as it has already invested no less than $62 billion in American stock, 20 of which during the first 6 months of 2016. See: Die Schweiz schluckt einen satten Teil der US-Börse, *Die Welt*, Frank Stocker, 22 August 2016.

[13]See: The Bank of Japan's Unstoppable Rise to Shareholder No. 1, Bloomberg, 14 August 2016.

Generally speaking, the objectives of these three central banks warrant comments. The first, price stability which, in the recent period, translated into the objective of generating inflation in order to reach a rate of 2%, instead of limiting it. This goal was achieved in the USA where the inflation rate was even at 2.11% in December 2017, but also associated with inflationary risks that should be considered. Within the Eurozone, this rate reached 1.5% in August 2017. In Japan, it was at 0.9% in December 2017.

In fact, inflation has found its place in the real estate and stock markets. In the latter, inflation has been accompanied by increased volatility. The discrepancy between market performance and the socio-economic situation is due to the large liquidity injections carried out by central banks into the financial sector.

The second is general and concerns financial sector stability and remains a so-called long-term objective in economist jargon, or in plain English, practically unattainable. In fact, those amounts injected into the financial sector contribute to the manipulation of interest rates as well as stock and bond prices, which results in the chronic instability of financial markets. The third, which concerns the FED, is full employment. According to official statistics, this objective is in the process of being accomplished, yet given the scale of concealed unemployment and underemployment, it seems rather long term.[14] The results, when compared with the objectives of the central banks, are limited. Furthermore, in the context of the current environmental, climate and social crisis, it seems to be an urgent task to reassess the objectives of central banks regarding their role in a sustainable economy.[15]

---

[14]See the preceding section in this same chapter entitled: *Devastating Effects of the Crisis.*

[15]See, e.g., http://unepinquiry.org/wp-content/uploads/2017/02/On_the_Role_of_Central_Banks_in_Enhancing_Green_Finance.pdf.

The Lure of the Banking Union

Let's return to Europe 1914 when the President of the French Republic, Raymond Poincaré, launched the formula of the "Sacred Union", repeated by numerous political figures: France "will be heroically defended by all its sons, whose sacred union will not break in the face of the enemy".[16] In 2014, it's about a totally different one in which the banking union is supposed to stabilise European banks and of which governments were proud. A great success it is indeed when an institution can only bail out, in the best of cases, two medium-sized banks which should only be able to function satisfactorily after 2025. Until the financial system is stable, composed of well-capitalised small banks, none of which considered systemic, this type of banking union will remain a wrong solution, especially useful for communication by the Brussels administration.[17] It is precisely this systemic character of the national banking champions that is dangerous as it encourages governments at certain critical moments to get taxpayers to bear their bailout costs rather than stockholders and bondholders: the pretext consists in wanting to limit the spread of default risk or bankruptcy.

Passing the bill on to them with no financial advantage whatsoever when they are not responsible for the difficulties of this or that bank is unjustifiable and leads to their impoverishment.

Protecting taxpayers and rendering stockholders and bondholders accountable would mean having a financial system consisting of smaller banks that assume responsibilities for their investment decisions, i.e. possibly going bankrupt if their strategy proves to be too risky.

---

[16]Poincaré, Raymond, *Au service de la France*, t. IV, Paris, Plon, 1927, p. 546.

[17]It has an annual communications budget of €500 million!

Austerity Plans

As referred to at the beginning of this chapter, trying to reassure financial markets means the implementation of austerity plans expected to be strict enough. If they not are perceived as such, these plans are presented as being too late or too weak. In order to keep the markets satisfied, is it really necessary to reduce workers' wages to the level of their Vietnamese or Indian counterparts, in order for Europe or the USA to improve its competitiveness? Surely not, such policies are extremely dangerous. They generate casual labour and a decline in wages. One wonders whether we have to go back to the early nineteenth century in order to please financial markets, i.e. to a time with no pension system and no social security...

Paradoxically, financial markets that focus as earnestly on labour costs should be alarmed at the abuses regarding compensation packages of various bank directors or CEOs of large companies (see the following chapter). They should also be concerned about cases of excessive dividends and the costs they represent for companies. They obviously do not analyse these problems with the same acuity.

The Dictatorship of the Financial Markets

Would daring to want to limit the influence of financial markets be seen as a sacrilege? Governments that attempt to satisfy financial markets that they present as being irrational, each time they react negatively to supposed good news, don't they themselves operate irrationally? Given that, as modern financial theory points out, financial markets often behave in an irrational manner, trying to satisfy them is not only illusory, but also encourages them to continue with this trend.

But who is hiding behind these financial markets, modern-age electronic gods the irrevocable sentences of whom appear on our screens in real time? More prosaically, they are powerful players such as investment banks and hedge funds that manipulate these same markets, or try to do so, in order to cash in on their bets. These dubious deals generate stock fluctuations, seemingly erratic, and lead the economy into a dangerous spiral.

To aim at reassuring financial markets dominated by these players is vain. When financial transactions are conducted at an increasingly faster rate, in a few microseconds for high-frequency trading, it is the feverishness of these stock markets and not their stability that produces unexpected gains.

Furthermore, the population feels evermore impotent. Political leaders are elected based on programmes which are very often undone as soon as they have the misfortune of displeasing financial markets. The power of the latter is contrary to the basic principles of democracy.

In 1966, during an Elysée press conference, General de Gaulle declared: "French policy is not made at the stock exchange".[18] We have no choice but to say the page has turned. Nowadays, electronic financial markets determine what the economic, financial and resulting social orientation of countries will be! The leaders, from both the left and right, usually apply one single policy, that of financial markets. This is a kind of dictatorship.

Greece Under Supervision

In early November 2011, Georgios Papandreou, Greek Prime Minister at the time, had the audacity to envisage a referendum which would allow his compatriots to give their opinion on the financial assistance that should be provided to their country and on the accompanying austerity plans. A few days later, he had lost power. Within a supposedly democratic framework, it would be desirable for citizens not only Greek but also German, French to have their say on the issues that concern them directly and to be able to decide on the use of public funds. In late 2014, the IMF announced that it would suspend its loans to this

---

[18]Declaration made at a press conference at the Élysée Palace on 28 October 1966.

country while awaiting the next government expected to be formed in January 2015. The European Union was also involved. Pierre Moscovici, European Commissioner for Economic and Financial Affairs regularly cautioned, "Greece must respect the engagements entered into and make the reforms imposed on it". For Wolfgang Schäuble, then German Minister of Finance, there was no alternative to the reforms set in place in Greece. Immediately after the elections, the rating agency Moody's declared that the Syriza party victory "had a negative influence on growth perspectives" of the economy (Reuters, 27 January 2015) and the President of the European Commission Jean-Claude Juncker advised, "there can be no democratic choice against European treaties". Troika, i.e. the European Commission, the European Central Bank and the IMF, has a particular conception of democracy: their demands should prevail over those of the voters. People can vote, but their governments should follow certain "recommendations". Otherwise, warnings then threats are sent to them, in particular to those who would be bold enough to envisage renegotiations and partial annulment of their debts, which mostly result from a policy logic promoted by international institutions and big banks.

On 25 January 2015, a new Greek government was elected based on a rejection of the dictatorship of the financial markets and the dictates of that Troika. Since that date, there has been no less than a rampant coup d'état.[19] Yanis Varoufakis, Greek finance minister, said in April 2015 "Our government must be prepared to confront a new type of coup d'état. Our assailants are no longer tanks, as they used to be in 1967, but banks". Among the assailants, one should include the Troika and rating agencies. A week after the no vote in the 5 July 2015 referendum, that is to say, the rejection of the injunctions from these institutions, the government finally confirmed the austerity policy of its predecessors. Greece and democracy were put under guardianship. In the absence of a real negotiation, the government elected in January 2015 had to actually consent to an unconditional surrender, namely

---

[19]See the article in *Le Monde* Diplomatique entitled: *Grèce, le coup d'Etat silencieux* dated June 2015 written by Stelios Kouloglou.

with many concessions, such as, not questioning the prior government's privatisation programme, suspending the planned increase of the minimum wage and increasing VAT. This policy often takes place at the expense of taxpayers, as illustrated by the sale "made by the Greek State in 2013, of twenty-eight buildings still used by it. Over the next twenty years Athens will have to pay €600 million in rent to the new private owners, representing almost the triple of the amount that it earned with the sale — that went directly to the creditors...".[20]

Also worth mentioning is the "privatisation" of 14 profitable Greek airports that served tourist destinations, which were sold off in 2015 to a quasi-German State enterprise Fraport-Slentel. It was the taxpayers who subsidised this transaction. In fact, this enterprise was allowed to use €300 million from European public funds to upgrade them, which Greece actually could have done to its advantage, had it not been forced to let them go.

Furthermore, the strict austerity policy seems to contain a noteworthy particularity.[21] The Tsipras government wanted to cut the defence budget by reducing military expenditure. The German and French governments insisted on the very opposite: decrease the staff budget rather than that allocated to arms. For those two countries, Greece represents a true opportunity. Germany exports submarines and, together with France, helicopters. The following example highlights this problem.

Already in 2000, the Greek government decided to buy three submarines from Germany, and in 2002, a fourth was ordered. The first one was delivered in 2010, with a delay of about 5 years. The total cost of this armament deal, that also included the renovation of the submarines already belonging to the Hellenic Republic, was €2.84 billion. It was known as the Archimedes programme. The first one was not operational on the delivery date as it was considered unfit for use by the Greek navy. In fact it pitched.

---

[20]Ibid.

[21]On this topic see: *Die Griechen haben nicht über ihre Verhältnisse gelebt*, Deutsche Wirtschafts Nachrichten, published on 7 August 2015.

In 2009, before the delivery, the Greek government had already paid 70% of the total and refused to pay the rest. In 2010, it launched an inquiry to throw light on this contract. This was also the case in Germany. The results showed that the signing of the agreement was tainted with payments of bribes in an amount of close to €55 million.

At the time this book is being written, this dispute has not yet been settled and Greece has paid approximately €2 billion to the German supplier, without ever having received a single submarine worthy of that name. One would believe them to be phantom submarines! Furthermore, the government's delay in reporting the deal's costs in the national accounts facilitated Greece's entry into the Eurozone.

To come back to the government elected in January 2015, it should be noted that it did not implement its programme. The future is bleak, and it is essential that another financial policy be applied given that the one used up to now is synonymous with failure. The population has suffered from a painful austerity regime which, economically speaking, has only served to worsen the situation. International institutions, such as the IMF, the ECB and the EU that want to come to Greece's rescue, have in fact helped German and French banks dispose of their Greek bad debt. In fact, up to 2008 these banks had loaned considerable amounts to this country and were in a delicate situation when its disastrous situation became all too apparent in 2009. At that time, the total amount of Greek debt was close to €300 billion. The financial sector was exposed at the rate of two-thirds this amount, i.e. approximately €200 billion. At the start of 2015, this sector did not hold more than 12% of Greek debt. More often than not they were vulture funds that sought to take advantage of the situation by demanding full reimbursement after having purchased these bonds at very low prices.[22]

It is likely a good deal for them and most definitely a bad one for European taxpayers. Between 2009 and 2015, the situation changed. In 2011, Jean-Claude Trichet, then President of the ECB, triggered a

---

[22]See article entitled: Grèce: retour sur six ans de politique européenne calamiteuse, published by *Mediapart* on 11 February 2015 and written by Martine Orange.

repurchase policy of securities from European countries in difficulty, Greece being one of them. The European Union and the ECB, both public institutions, are in the forefront as regards exposure to Greek debt. In February 2012, it was restructured and 53% of the total held by private creditors, i.e. €107 billion, was wiped out.

In fact, tens of billions of euros in compensation in the form of recapitalisations and public guarantees were granted to these creditors[23] and, in particular, to the big French and German banks who agreed to accept this write-off. Therefore, the above-mentioned European institutions organised the socialisation of losses. On behalf of what do European taxpayers have to assume the risks taken by these big banks? To the satisfaction of financial markets!

Only around 10% of the nearly €300 billion in public aid spent within the framework of "bail-out" plans benefitted Greece. The rest returned to the hands of the creditors.

A partial cancellation of the enormous debt of this country, approximately €320 billion in 2017, seems inevitable. This was the case for Germany in 1953 which, after the war, had a debt of around 200% of its GDP. However, the ECB and the EU continue to refute the evidence. The IMF only recognised it "a little late" in early July 2015,[24] after having kept up an intransigent attitude during "negotiations" with Greece. On the contrary and for some time now, from February 2014, the IMF has been much more flexible with Ukraine, also faced with a catastrophic financial situation. The IMF's decision-making criteria manifestly followed the principle of variable geometry.

---

[23]Ibid.

[24]See: *Greece: An Update of IMF Staff's Preliminary Public Debt Sustainability Analysis*, IMF Country Report No. 15/186, 14 July 2015.

Who Are They Trying to Fool?

Do the markets have virtues that oblige the States to keep the books for them? Really, that would be trickery, as the Greek example illustrates. Its budgetary slippages were partly camouflaged in 2000 thanks to the use of a complex financial product, the *currency swap*,[25] set up by an important player in these markets, the bank Goldman Sachs, in this case. This questionable financial structure costs Greece at least €300 million in commissions for this bank. Among other things, thanks to this hidden amount of debt, this country was able to apparently meet the Maastricht criteria and therefore become part of the Eurozone, which should never have occurred. Mario Draghi, the current President of the European Central Bank, was Vice-President of Goldman Sachs International from 2002 to 2005. It should be noted that he has never publicly condemned these operations. Lucas Papademos, then Governor of the Greek central bank and Prime Minister of the country in 2011, was a key figure in the transaction. These two leaders were, or are still part, on the date this book is being written, of this group of technocrats who in Europe are supposed to put public accounts back into order and limit the size of debts.

Furthermore, the ECB refuses to disclose the information it has with regard to these dubious practices. Bloomberg wished to have access to the two analyses conducted by ECB experts that covered the period from 1998 to 2001. The ECB's decision was confirmed by the European Court of Justice ruling dated 29 November 2012 that rejected Bloomberg's request and authorised it to hide the information. According to the European Court, "Disclosing these documents would have harmed the protection of the public interest with regard to the economic policy of the European Union and Greece".

---

[25]Currency swaps: These are financial contracts obliging the parties concerned to exchange amounts of foreign currency at a certain exchange rate and on a certain date and to subsequently proceed to the corresponding interest payments and the final reimbursement of the amounts in question. In the case we are interested in, the currency swap and the use of a euro dollar exchange rate allowed Greece to make a concealed loan, in the sense that it did not appear in the national accounts.

How could the disclosure of documents coming from a public institution harm public interest? In the name of what would such an institution, in this case the ECB, be authorised to give a confidential nature to its analyses of the key period preceding the creation of the euro? What are the secrets it wants to hide? Citizens should have access to this information because they are the ones paying the bill for these questionable deals carried out by Goldman Sachs. What did the ECB know, or did not want to know, about these? What are the Members of the European Parliament waiting for to seize the dossier?

Breaking the Taboo of Financial Markets' Excessive Size and Complexity

Henry Ford, founder of the Ford Motor Company said in his time: "It is well enough that people of the nation do not understand our banking and monetary system. For if they did, I believe there would be a revolution before tomorrow morning".

Given its dimension and opacity, the financial sector effectively endeavours to protect itself from democratic control.

Derivatives,[26] complex by construction, have become an essential component of financial markets. In the case of currencies for example, they are usually presented as hedging instruments allowing real economy players, such as importers and exporters, to protect themselves against unfavourable variations in exchange rates. For example, if a UK company imports products manufactured in Switzerland, it will have to complete settlement in Swiss francs on a given date. A hedge against a possible increase of the franc vis-à-vis the pound might be useful in order to avoid suffering serious consequences, i.e. to purchase francs at a higher price. An airline could protect itself against a possible increase in fuel prices by acquiring call options on it and allowing it to pay for such fuel at a price in dollars established in advance.

---

[26]Derivatives: financial contracts the value of which depends on an underlying asset. For example, a call option on a stock allows its holder to buy a share at a fixed price in advance and during a predetermined period of time.

Derivatives have a nominal value globally that represents around 8 times the world's GDP. This is completely oversized. The importer does not need to hedge 8 times the value of the purchased products, but only once. Likewise, the airline company does not need to hedge 8 times its fuel volume, but only once. Furthermore, many economic sectors, like many services, are not highly susceptible to sudden price variations. For example, the translation of a book very seldom requires protection against any eventual changes in fees.

If derivatives essentially corresponded to insurance products, their nominal value would be much lower than that of global GDP, around 20 or 40% of it, and not 8 times higher!

Derivatives also constitute a dimension of the Greek question. One of the reasons the IMF, the ECB and the EU were so obstinate in denying the evidence of a Greek bankruptcy was because of the enormous amount of financial products in circulation, enabling bets on such a bankruptcy. We are talking about Credit Default Swaps that will be explained in Chapter 4. As these products are treated in an extremely opaque fashion and with no real regulation, the authorities in charge are not able or do not really want to know whether it was banks in Frankfurt, Paris, London or New York that sold these contracts. By denying this bankruptcy, the activation of these bets was prevented, and the banks that sold them avoided finding themselves in a delicate situation. As an example, Deutsche Bank could have been truly shaken by a Greek default. In fact, as shown in Chapter 4, its derivative activities are disproportionate. Furthermore, the indebtedness of this bank is enormous. The risks it takes are also particularly significant. In particular, if it turns out that it has sold vast amounts of bets on a Greek default, its losses could be catastrophic if Greece fails to repay its debt.

Exchange markets are also excessive in terms of size. A week of transactions on these markets would be sufficient to allow for the yearly amount of international trade of goods and services to be conducted. What is the economic use of these transactions during the remaining 51 weeks? They contribute to the development of uncontrolled speculation that damages the efficiency and transparency of foreign exchange markets, essential for companies in their import–export activities. On 15 January 2015, the announcement of the abandonment of the 1.2 francs to euro minimum rate, by the Swiss National

Bank (SNB), was also the result of the immoderate size of foreign exchange markets. The SNB established such a rate in 2011 with the objective to fight the franc's trend of continuous appreciation. In order to maintain this policy, it had to buy enormous amounts of euros. The cost of this policy has thus become too high.[27] To put this into perspective, in 2013 the average daily volume of all the transactions in francs corresponded to close to $270 billion, 70 of which for the franc-euro exchange.[28] A hedge fund pledging $500 million may obtain a loan of $9.5 billion from a major credit bank. A 5% initial commitment is enough. It can therefore heavily speculate on a rise in the franc and a drop in the euro: $10 billion. Other hedge funds and big banks can do the same. Long term, it is difficult for the SNB to compete with such players. Its balance sheet was already approximately CHF 500 billion just before this announcement, i.e. close to 85% of Swiss GDP. It could not let it grow indefinitely by buying billions of euros sold by hedge funds or big banks every day, in order to try to limit the rise in the franc. Furthermore, how could these euros be invested wisely? The assets associated with a currency, the future of which is uncertain, pose very high risks.

Complexity, on the other hand, is a true factor of both profit and power: of profit, because investment banks in a position to issue complex derivatives[29] in fact exclude their smaller competitors from this market, thus hoping to make large profits. Complexity is also a power factor as only the heads of investment banks or hedge funds are assumed to understand and master such complexity. There are many who go on to occupy the highest political positions. This is the case of former heads of Goldman Sachs, such as Robert E. Rubin and Henry M. Paulson Jr., who both subsequently became Treasury Secretary under the Clinton and Obama administrations, respectively. It is also the case of Mario Draghi, mentioned above, who is at the time this book is being written, President of the European Central Bank, of Mark Carney, his homolog in England, of William Dudley, Director of the

---

[27]See the article entitled: La décision de la BNS en dix questions, written by Frédéric Lelièvre and published by the newspaper *Le Temps* on 7 September 2011.

[28]See the Bank for International Settlements report: Triennial Central Bank Survey Global foreign exchange market turnover in 2013, February 2014.

[29]These products might facilitate insider trading activities. See the scientific article entitled: Detecting Abnormal Trading Activities in Option Markets, written by Marc Chesney, Remo Crameri and Loriano Mancini and published in the *Journal of Empirical Finance* in 2015.

Federal Reserve Bank of New York[30] as well as of Mario Monti, Prime Minister of the Italian Government from 2011 to 2013, who all held senior positions at Goldman Sachs. The Director of the Banque de France appointed in September 2015, François Villeroy de Galhau, was still deputy CEO of the group BNP Paribas shortly before this date.

The Spanish Minister for the Economy, Luis de Guindos, appointed in late 2011, cannot be left out, as he was President of Lehman Brothers Bank for the Iberian Peninsula.

These technocrats presented as being neutral more often than not set up policies favourable to the institutions they belonged to or that they will belong to, as is the case of José Manuel Barroso, former President of the European Commission, who in 2016 was hired by Goldman Sachs as consultant and non-executive chairman, as well as Philipp Hildebrand, former head of the SNB who is now a vice chairman of BlackRock!

In fact, the overwhelming majority of the population is excluded from the debate on risks associated with financial markets and financial innovation. It is a great concern for democracy and for taxpayers in particular, as they are ultimately the ones who bear the risks!

In conclusion, in the current situation, attempting to please the financial Moloch is not only vain but also dangerous in social, democratic, economic and environmental terms. The financial sector enslaves society and imposes its logic on the economy that is not in a position to play its role and allow further development of the human society.

At this level it is interesting to analyse how the financial sphere, wearing the clothes of liberal doctrine, presumed to meet the interests of the majority, contradicts the principles of this doctrine day after day by engaging in a dynamic that is far from democratic. The financial oligarchy finds support in extremely powerful lobbies[31] that have the power to influence governments and international institutions. Contradictions between the virtuous principles proclaimed by the financial sector and the dubious manner in which it operates are the topics of the next chapter.

---

[30]In the United States, the 12 Regional Reserve Banks, New York included, belong to private banks.

[31]To this regard see: Simon Johnson and James Kwak, *13 Bankers, The Wall Street Takeover and the Next Financial Meltdown*, New York, Pantheon Books, 2010.

Bibliography

Bank for International Settlements Report: Triennial Central Bank Survey Global Foreign Exchange Market Turnover in 2013, February 2014.

Greece: *An Update of IMF Staff's Preliminary Public Debt Sustainability Analysis*, IMF Country Report No. 15/186, 14 July 2015.

Kraus, Karl, *The Last Days of Mankind*, Yale University Press, USA, 2015.

Musil, Robert, *The Man Without Qualities*, Vintage, USA, 1996.

Nyborg, Kjell G.: *Collateral Frameworks: The Open Secret of Central Banks*, Cambridge University Press, 2017.

Poincaré, Raymond, *Au service de la France*, Paris, Plon, 1927.

3

Liberalism: The Financial Sphere Does Not Practice What It Preaches

During the golden century of liberalism, from the end of the Napoleonic wars to the outbreak of the First World War, the development of industrial nations was supported by the existence of major banks that helped national industries to benefit from local savings. With the first globalisation, during the period between 1870 and 1914,[1] the process became international in the sense that these financial establishments increasingly geared national savings towards other countries. France was then at the peak of its international investments, immediately after the UK.[2]

This chapter and the following are partly based on my article entitled Der Liberalismus und die Logik des Finanzsektors, *Neue Zürcher Zeitung*, 1 July 2013.

---

[1] With regard to this subject, see the work: *Notre première mondialisation*. Leçons d'un échec oublié, Suzanne Berger, Paris, République des Idées, Seuil, 2003.

[2] Ibid., Online English version, p. 4.

© The Author(s) 2018
M. Chesney, *A Permanent Crisis*,
https://doi.org/10.1007/978-3-030-00518-4_3

When certain banks started to shift savings towards questionable rather than productive investments, the latter were transformed into write-offs. The Panama Canal Scandal[3] is a perfect example of this. The Russian loans, another: long before the 1917 revolution, voices were raised to warn about the situation that prevailed in that empire. According to a Russian economist of the time,[4] the budget of that country was "a decorative object for foreign benefit". In France, Jean Jaurès denounced the monopolistic control of French savings left in the hands of a few banks, as well as the commissions that they collected for their loans abroad. The scale of profits was particularly important. For Crédit Lyonnais, for example, between 1887 and 1903, 30% of its profits came from costs imposed on clients for participating in these loans.[5] Overly good-hearted journalists touted the benefits of these investments to the delight of certain French banks.[6] What happened next is well known. At the end of the First World War, two-thirds of French investments abroad were purely and simply lost.[7]

From the First to the Second Globalisation

Globalisation requires the freest as possible movement of people, goods and capital and presupposes technological advancement which enables this to take place.

During the first globalisation, these movements relied on the railway and maritime sectors, as well as on the telegraph and telephone. With the second, starting in the 1980s, it relied on airline and space industries, as well as on the Internet which replaced the telegraph. The

---

[3]The **Panama Scandal**: It was a scandal related to corruption in France in the late nineteenth century. Because of it, a French company, formed in 1879 to fund the construction of the Panama Canal, went bankrupt in 1889.

[4]See the English version of the work cited above, p. 65.

[5]Ibid., p. 51.

[6]Ibid., p. 63.

[7]Ibid., p. 39.

underlying technologies are IT and artificial intelligence, among others. The globalisation of exchanges and interconnection between countries is no guarantor of peace or stability. The first globalisation was shattered by the First World War. The second has not settled the numerous tensions and imbalances that currently exist and has triggered many crises in the financial sector and beyond.

Nowadays, the economic Eldorado is no longer Russian, it is Chinese, and the major Western banks are directly involved in the organisation and implementation of foreign investments in that country. The issue now is that it is highly probable that the economic, social and environmental risks have been underestimated and the information incomplete. The USA also plays a key role within the framework of this second globalisation. It incarnates another Eldorado: this time a reference for unbridled neoliberalism. After the 1980s, Wall Street sets the tone for finance in terms of opaque and dubious structures as well as toxic assets towards which savings have been diverted. Investors thus entrapped had to pay the bill. Furthermore, this country's military power and the dollar's dominance guarantee it a certain advantage and allow it to continue to live beyond its means.

This second globalisation, unlike the first, harms social progress and poses an increasing threat to natural habitats and ecosystems. Its main feature is that it is under the sway of casino finance and that it suffers from a growing gap between the logic of the financial sector and the needs of the economy and society. The situation worsens from one generation to another, and public fear is ever growing. The neoliberal agenda taken on board in the 1980s and the role devolved to big banks in this process are key elements in this globalisation which deserves careful analysis.

The 1970s characterised by stagflation,[8] the collapse of the Bretton Woods Agreement that had guaranteed fixed exchange rates between principal currencies since the end of the Second World War, the

---

[8]Economic situation where economic stagnation, meaning sluggish even negative growth, is accompanied by inflation.

economic consequences of the Vietnam War and the oil crises, marked the end of an era. With Margaret Thatcher's coming to power in the UK in 1979 and Ronald Reagan in the USA in 1981, the 1980s would witness a change in international economic policies. *Supply-side policies* replaced *demand-side policies of a Keynesian nature*, which are based on an interventionist state whose spending is supposed to regulate the economy and keep unemployment low.

Supply-side policies are neoliberal by nature, based on the deregulation of the economic and financial spheres as well as on the privatisation of government owned enterprises. It is accompanied by a monetary policy, the purpose of which is to contain inflation. A central bank supposedly independent of political power is meant to control the money supply. These policies are supposed to create the conditions that lead to subsequent economic growth.

This deregulation logic led to implicit rules such as those conferring rating agencies with an exorbitant power on the economy, or those allowing financial institutions supposed to be "too big to fail" to fund themselves at lower cost—which at the end of the day essentially corresponds to allocating them subsidies—or still those requiring taxpayers to pay the costs linked to eventual bailouts of these same institutions when they are in a situation of near bankruptcy.

Cartels, the use of subsidies, the privatisation of profits and the socialisation of losses are clearly contrary to the spirit of liberalism.

What Is Liberalism?

Here, we want to show that the financialisation of the economy, which characterises the current globalisation, contradicts the basic principles of liberalism on which it is supposed to be based. Considering a few authors who are references in this area such as Ludwig Von Mises, Friedrich August von Hayek, Milton Friedman and Adam Smith and their contributions, will help us focus more closely on what liberalism should be.

First of all von Mises who to the question "what is liberalism?" replies:

Liberalism is a doctrine directed entirely towards the conduct of men in this world. In the last analysis, it has nothing else in view than the advancement of their outward, material welfare.[9] And he proceeds as follows, "Historically, liberalism was the first political movement that aimed at promoting the welfare of all, not that of special groups.[10]

To the question on knowing what liberalism is not, von Mises replies:

Antiliberal policy is a policy of capital consumption. It recommends that the present be more abundantly provided for at the expense of the future.[11]

For his part, Friedrich von Hayek expresses himself very clearly against government interventionism in economic affairs and what liberalism should avoid. He writes:

The state should confine itself to establishing rules applying to general types of situations, and should allow the individuals freedom in everything which depends on the circumstances of time and place, because only the individuals concerned in each instance can fully know these circumstances and adapt their actions to them.[12]

Finally, according to Adam Smith, in a liberal society everyone "led by an invisible hand to promote an end which was no part of his intention" [...]. "By pursuing his own interest he frequently promotes that of the society more effectually than when he really intends to promote it".[13] In other words, in trying to satisfy his own interests one promotes those of society. Adam Smith's concept of the "invisible hand" expresses this idea.

---

[9]Mises, Ludwig von, *Liberalism*, Cobden Press, USA, 2002, Introduction, p. 4.
[10]Ibid., Introduction, p. 7.
[11]Ibid., p. 9.
[12]Hayek, Friedrich August von, *The Road to Serfdom*, Routledge, USA, 1944, p. 79.
[13]Smith, Adam, *An Inquiry into the Nature and Causes of the Wealth of Nations*, London, Methuen & Co., Ltd., 1904.

Globally, from the end of the Napoleonic wars to the onset of the First World War, the implementation of policies inspired by liberalism has allowed for unprecedented development in both economic and scientific as well as social domains, and for a greater number of people.

A Financial Oligarchy Dressed in Liberal Clothing

Comparing each of the preceding extracts with the current situation is particularly instructive. Let's start with von Mises.

> Historically, liberalism was the first political movement that aimed at promoting the welfare of all, not that of special groups.

The income distribution allows to measure whether general welfare is being respected or neglected. This is where a historic perspective is needed. According to the economist Thomas Piketty,[14] in 1910 in the USA the 1% of the population with the highest income received approximately 18% of total remunerations. In 1970, the situation found a partial re-balance as that same 1% received 8% of total compensations. In 2010, income disparities were once again very high, i.e. 18% of total remunerations received by 1% of the population and corresponded to the situation 100 years earlier.

Now, if instead of focusing on that 1% of the population with the highest income, a still lower percentage of around 0.01% is considered, then in comparison with the First World War, disparities are even greater. At this point, it is worthwhile to mention that the works by Thomas Piketty are based on tax declarations; the existence of tax havens, complex financial structures and opaque accounting techniques makes it easier to camouflage vast incomes and fortunes. The situation, even with such make-up, is clear. In numerous countries, differences in income have reached extreme and unprecedented levels today.

---

[14]Piketty, Thomas, *Capital in the Twenty-First Century*, Harvard University Press, 2014.

The case of the USA speaks for itself. In 2006, the twenty best paid hedge fund managers received $657 million on average. This income is close to 15,000 times higher than that year's average salary. The ratio between the highest remunerations and the average salary was around 30–40 in 1970. This hedge fund managers' average income corresponded to 18 times the average salary of the 20 best paid CEOs of non-financial institutions on the S&P 500 index, which shows where real power lies.

In terms of comparison, in France, the ratio between the salary of the President of the Republic and that of minimum wage earners is around 10.[15] In 2006, Thierry Desmarest, the Chairman of the Board of Total, received close to €3 million, i.e. 2142 times more than a minimum wage earner received.

In 2006, the CEO of the Renaissance Technologies hedge fund received $1.5 billion, i.e. close to twenty times more than the best compensated CEO of non-financial institution on the S&P 500 index, in this case, the President of Yahoo with $72 million.

In 2007, this multiple reached 44. John Paulson, CEO of his eponymous hedge fund, in fact received around $3.7 billion while the best compensated CEO of non-financial institution, namely Oracle's CEO, made $85 million. For Mr. Paulson, this amount represents approximately 80,000 times the average income in the USA.

In 2013, the gaps grew even bigger in relation to 2007. The twenty best paid CEOs of hedge funds received on average $1.1 billion, i.e. close to 25,000 times the average salary in this country and 33 times more than the average of the 20 highest salaries of CEOs of non-financial institutions on the S&P 500 index, in this case $33 million. In that same year, George Soros, CEO of Soros Fund Management Renaissance Technologies hedge fund, beat every record. He received an amount of $4 billion, i.e. approximately 52 times more than Larry Ellison, the best paid CEO (Oracle) of non-financial institutions on the S&P 500 index,

---

[15]In fact, the real gap is greater as the President of the Republic resides at the Elysée Palace at taxpayers' expense and pays no utility bills: accommodation, food, trips...

who received $76.9 million[16] and around 87,000 times more than the average income in the USA.

In 2016, the highest paid hedge fund managers, James Simmons and Michel Platt, managers of Renaissance Technologies Corp. and Bluecrest Capital Management, respectively, received an income of $1.5 billion each. This corresponds to approximately 34,000 times the average income in the USA[17] and 6.3 more than the income of CEO of Walmart, Marc Lore, the highest paid CEO of non-financial institutions on the S&P 500 index, who received $237 million.

Regarding the CEO of Goldman Sachs, in 2016 he made $20.2 million. The party goes on for the financial oligarchy.

From a liberal perspective, this type of astronomical compensations is even more problematic and unjustifiable if it is accompanied by heavy losses for the shareholder and taxpayer.

Brady Dougan, for example, at the head of Credit Suisse until early March 2015, during his eight years as CS CEO, received around CHF 160 million whereas during that same period the CS share price lost close to 70% of its value and this bank, accused of having facilitated tax evasion in the USA, had to pay a record fine of $2.8 billion! Not only did this fine affect shareholders as well as clients up to a certain extent, but it also affected taxpayers as this amount was partially deducted from the bank's taxes! The situation did not improve with his successor Tidjane Thiam who earned around CHF 19 million in 2015, despite a CS share price loss of 60% of its value between July 2015 and July 2016. In 2016, he received CHF 11.9 million, although "a near-3 billion franc loss at Credit Suisse amid a major restructuring and penalties for the sale of toxic mortgage debt in the run-up to the financial crisis".[18]

---

[16]See the link: http://graphics.wsj.com/executive-salary-compensation-2014/, Executive Compensation: How CEOs Rank, *Wall Street Journal*.

[17]See: Forbes, Bureau of Labour Statistics, 2018.

[18]See: Credit Suisse CEO Pockets $12 Million Despite Back-to-Back Losses, *Business News*, 24 March 2017.

UBS is no exception because if the bonuses paid out during the difficult years of 2007, 2008, 2009 and 2012 had been suppressed, it would have recovered a good part of its losses. This bank should have paid taxes on its profits from 2012 instead of waiting till 2017. The loss in tax-generated income for the Canton of Zurich is approximately CHF 49 million, i.e. almost exactly what this canton, and in particular its education system, needed to save in 2017![19] It should be recalled that the Swiss taxpayer was called to the rescue in 2008 to avoid a bankruptcy of UBS and that bonuses paid at that time were particularly unjustifiable.

Richard Fuld, ex-CEO of Lehman Brothers, received close to a half a billion dollars between 2000 and 2007 despite his responsibility in the strategy that would lead this bank to bankruptcy.

There are many examples of this type and in different geographies. For example, in Spain one of the CEOs of Bankia, Aurelio Izquierdo, received a "golden parachute" of €7.6 million in 2012 for his future retirement, despite the €23 billion that European taxpayers had to pay this bank to ensure it would not go bankrupt.

As far as the former CEO of AIG Financial Product Division Joseph Cassano is concerned, after his retirement in 2008 he stayed on as a "consultant" for a salary of $1 million a month. This company almost went bust in 2008 and was bailed out by the American taxpayer. According to him, this consultancy contract would help keep his "intellectual knowledge" in AIG![20] Contrary to other financial institutions, AIG had massively bet on the survival of Lehman Brothers, which was at the source of its problems. What "intellectual knowledge" are we talking about? *That is the question.*

Reference should also be made to Jamie Dimon, CEO of JPMorgan Chase, whose earnings increased by 74% in 2013 to total $20 million despite losses of close to $6 billion resulting from the activities of trader Bruno Iksil in 2012 referred to in Chapter 1, and the $20 billion in penalties paid by this bank in 2013 in order to try to find a solution

---

[19]Cf. *Bessere Bildung statt hohe Boni*, Marc Chesney and Brigitte Maranghino-Singer, *Tagesanzeiger*, 30 December 2015.

[20]See Joseph Cassano's participation in the film *Inside Job*.

for the multiple court cases and accusations they were faced with, one of which being complicity in fraud in the case of the crook Bernard Madoff. Benefitting from an understanding management board and running a so-called too big to fail bank is clearly very profitable.

According to von Mises, in a liberal society, in a given sector, only overall growth of labour productivity can generate salary increases. As regards the financial world, to argue that the level reached by the highest remunerations would be justified by growth in productivity, reveals, in view of the numerous problems and inequalities associated with the crisis, intellectual dishonesty if not cynicism.[21]

Statistics regarding the world's most economically deprived people are also just as striking. According to the Pew Research Center, some 71% of the world's population had less than ten dollars per day at its disposal at the beginning of the twenty-first century and were therefore considered to be poor or low income. According to the FAO, close to 800 million individuals suffered from the consequences of chronic malnutrition in 2014 and over three million children die of such consequences every year.

Such accumulated wealth also sheds light on these unjustifiable gaps. According to Forbes Magazine, in 2017 the world's accumulated hundred largest fortunes corresponded to $2.3 trillion.[22] Furthermore, in 2015 the one per cent of the world's richest population possessed as much as the remaining 99% of the population, meaning 50% of the world's wealth. Finally, according to the British NGO OXFAM, in 2016 the 8 wealthiest individuals owned as much as the poorest half of the world's population and in 2017, "Eighty two percent of the wealth generated went to the richest one percent of the global population, while the 3.7 billion people who make up the poorest half of the world saw no increase".

---

[21]In terms of average productivity of the financial sector per employee, in Switzerland this corresponds to only half of that of the pharmaceutical sector. See: Pharmafirmen schlagen Banken, Birgit Volgt, *NZZ am Sonntag*, 29 January 2017.

[22]See: *The List*. 2017 Ranking, Forbes, 2018.

Thus at the international level, the huge gaps that we observe in terms of both income and wealth are comparable to those that existed before the First World War, even worse still. They are the symptoms of the insatiable bulimia of the financial sector and the logic that it imposes on that of the economy. This pathology is humanely detrimental, as it is contrary to the basic principles and values, learnt by most people from their earliest childhood, irrespective of their origin, culture or possible religion, and which constitute the basis of their education. This increasing disconnect between a small and wealthy financial elite and a broad part of the population leaving in conditions of scarcity is also economically harmful. Our society is hostage to powerful lobbies that try, not without success, to persuade citizens that the economy would never be able to function efficiently without this unjustifiable system that sees CEOs of certain companies, in particular financial, making dozens of millions of dollars a year. These sums are even more scandalous as the biggest financial institutions are in part financed by taxpayers, as will be highlighted in the next chapter. Much lower earnings of around 1 million dollars a year would appear to be less unreasonable.[23]

Albeit still very high, they would correspond to the compensation gaps observed after the Second World War and up to the 1970s, a time during which the world economy was more stable and the unemployment rate lower.

Always going to the highest bidder and changing countries or continents whenever a better opportunity presents itself, highlights the irresponsibility of the leaders who do this. It corresponds rather to the model of a soccer star, disconnected from the context in which he evolves. Cleaning up the current economy requires another kind of mindset.

---

[23]In the UK, for example, a study showed that it is positive for shareholders and companies when CEOs are paid sensibly. See: CEO Compensation and Future Shareholder Returns: Evidence from London Stock Exchange, Nick Balafas and Chris Florackis, *Journal of Empirical Finance*, 2014.

The principle announced by Ludwig von Mises, "liberalism has always had the general welfare in mind, and not the welfare of a particular group", is clearly not respected.

A Colossal Level of Debt

Let's continue with another quotation by von Mises:

> Antiliberal policy is a policy of capital consumption. It recommends that the present be more abundantly provided for at the expense of the future.

The extent to which financial and fiscal policies benefit the present to the detriment of the future can be assessed in debt levels. The same can be said for individual debt. Within a family, accumulated debt affects future generations who, sooner or later, will be supposed to pay the bill.

In 2014, total debt, by which is meant that of individuals, non-financial companies, the State and the financial sector in the USA on the one hand and in Germany on the other, reached 269 and 258% of GDP, respectively.[24] Other developed countries have similar or even worse statistics. In late 2016, China's debt exceeded 280%. At the end of the third quarter of 2017, global debt was at least 300% of world GDP and was growing faster than the latter. It is very difficult to imagine how such a level of debt could ever be paid! The too big to fail banks are also highly indebted. In a number of countries, not only Greece, but also the UK and the USA, there is less and less income tax to build schools and hospitals or to pay civil servants' pensions as it is increasingly used for interest payments on public debt! This situation will worsen if interest rates increase. In 2016, in Italy, for example, annual interest on public debt was close to €70 billion. If rates increase, the situation might become unsustainable. To give an example, the health budget corresponds to €113 billion. In a country like Nigéria, debt service was already 30 times higher than the Health Ministry's 2017 budget.[25]

---

[24]Source: *MGI Country Debt Database*, McKinsey Global Institute Analysis.
[25]Source: Es ist fünf vor zwölf in Afrika, Fabian Urech, *NZZ*, 20 February 2018.

The implementation of the neoliberal doctrine is mainly responsible for this colossal level of indebtedness. It suffices to quote Milton Friedman to convince ourselves of this: "By concentrating on the wrong thing, the deficit, instead of the right thing, total government spending, fiscal conservatives have been the unwitting handmaidens of the big spenders".[26] According to Friedman, the main objective should not be to decrease deficits but rather taxes. Neoliberal logic would hope for such a decrease to encourage the State to spend less and limit its interventions which would result in deficit reduction. Over thirty years of experience of this type of policy shows that the drop in taxes afforded to more affluent households and to large companies has not had the desired effect. On the contrary, deficits have ballooned.

Within the context of the current financialised economy, debt has become a decisive factor of economic growth, which results in making the latter less sustainable. Indeed, between 2001 and 2005, the average yearly increase of the total amount of public and private debt was substantial in the USA and the UK: 6.5 and 8.3%, respectively, which had the effect of stimulating economic growth, the yearly average of which was 2.4 and 3%, respectively, in these two countries.

During this period, growth had been clearly weaker in a country like Germany, i.e. 0.6%, while debts had only increased by 2.3%. France is at an intermediary level with 1.6%, and its debt suffers a yearly increase of 5.1%.

The onset of the financial crisis revealed the superficial nature of this growth. The importance given over to debt and the short-term speculative bets associated with it are, instead of long-term savings and investments, characteristic of the increasing power of a casino economy and its dangers.

These traits and in particular the levels of public and private debt are not compatible with a balanced and sustainable ratio between the present and the future. In fact, the current policy incontestably favours the present at the expense of the future.

---

[26]Friedman, Milton, The Limitations of Tax Limitation, *Policy Review*, 1978, p. 11.

As to State *interventionism*, criticised by Friedrich Hayek, the conclusion is obvious; it is currently being implemented, not in the sense analysed by this author, but essentially in terms of the bailout of financial institutions that are "too big to fail" or "too connected to fail". This policy has devoured huge sums and is contrary to the logic of liberalism. Indeed, according to the latter, all institutions should be responsible for their strategic decisions and none should have an a priori guarantee of being allowed to avoid possible bankruptcy. This policy favours strategies that consist in reaching such a critical size and playing such a key role within the financial network that they benefit from public protection.

Finally, the invisible hand of Adam Smith is increasingly less effective in the financial realm. Trying to satisfy their own interests is less and less compatible with those of society. Issuing so-called structured financial products, usually meaning complex and toxic, damages the economy and therefore the general welfare of society.

The big banks that are active in this field behave like pyromaniac firefighters. In fact, the dissemination of these products, which is supposed to help reduce risks for the client, actually generates them at the global level. Such financial bets can only be made to the detriment of their clients. There cannot be bets satisfying both parties, as logically, one will win at the expense of the other. Given the amounts spent by big banks to advertise them, the reader will easily guess whom they normally benefit.[27] To illustrate these problems, two examples of structured products are shown in the following chapter.

One can clearly see that the financial sector stands in contradiction to the principles it is meant to respect and promote. Based on several specific cases, a number of salient features of casino finance will now be highlighted.

---

[27]And moreover, these financial institutions usually hedge these operations, which allows them to charge (high and opaque) fees on these products to the detriment of their clients without running any risk.

Bibliography

Berger, Suzanne, *Notre première mondialisation*. Leçons d'un échec oublié, Paris, République des Idées, Seuil, 2003.

Friedman, Milton, The Limitations of Tax Limitation, *Policy Review*, 1978.

Hayek, Friedrich August von, *The Road to Serfdom*, Routledge, USA, 1944.

Mises, Ludwig von, *Liberalism*, Cobden Press, USA, 2002.

Piketty, Thomas, *Capital in the Twenty-First Century*, Harvard University Press, 2014.

Smith, Adam, *An Inquiry into the Nature and Causes of the Wealth of Nations*, London, Methuen & Co., Ltd., 1904.

The List. 2017 Ranking, Forbes, 2018.

4

Characteristics of Casino Finance

The economist John Maynard Keynes stated in 1936 that, "When the capital development of a country becomes a by-product of the activities of a casino, the job is likely to be ill-done".[1] The current situation is even worse as the real actors of this unbridled finance—big banks and hedge funds—not only bet at the casino but often do so with money that does not belong to them, but rather to taxpayers, pensioners, clients and of course shareholders!

As analysed in the preceding chapter, numerous characteristics of the financial sector contradict the basic principles of liberalism and of a market economy. The modus operandi of this sector and the complex financial products it issues are often problematic, and this is the subject of this chapter.

---

[1]Keynes, John Maynard, *The General Theory of Employment, Interest and Money*, Macmillan Cambridge University Press, 1936.

© The Author(s) 2018
M. Chesney, *A Permanent Crisis*,
https://doi.org/10.1007/978-3-030-00518-4_4

The Stock Exchange at the Speed of Light and Liar's Poker

Currently in the USA, according to various sources, on average, an investor holds a share for a few minutes, whereas in 1940, it would be held for approximately five years. This order of magnitude, ridiculously low, is explained mainly by the automation of stock exchange transactions that allows powerful banks to conduct their financial transactions in an extremely short period of time of a few milliseconds or even millionths of a second and done with the assistance of ultra-powerful computers. However, the main purpose of the stock exchange is to allow for optimal allocation of capital and risks: this task has obviously not been accomplished.

The stock exchange is supposed to allow companies to finance themselves. This is increasingly no longer the case. In France, for example, traded companies were able, in 2011, to raise money on the equity markets for only 5.4% of their needs, which is very low! In 2001, the percentage was still at 27%. In Belgium, a similar low percentage was also observed for non-financial enterprises. During the period 1995–2005, the stock markets only contributed up to 5% of funding sources.[2] In order to generate such limited financing, it would be enough for the exchanges to open one hour a week![3]

According to Thomas Peterffy, founder of Interactive Brokers Group Inc, "the stock exchange has become a gigantic casino. Except for the fact that a casino functions in a more transparent manner and is easier to understand".[4] The development of high-frequency

---

[2]Source: www.dealogic.com for France and Le rôle des actions dans le financement des societes en Belgique, *Revue économique*, Banque Nationale de Belgique, September 2006, authors: V. Baugnet and G. Wuyts.

[3]See article entitled: Arrêtons la cotation en temps continu sur les marchés, published by the newspaper *Le Monde* on 26 November 2012 written by authors: Marc Chesney, Denis Dupré and Ollivier Taramasco.

[4]Launched at the opening of the annual meeting of market operators, the World Federation of Exchange (WFE) in Paris, Monday, 11 October 2010, continued in an article by Claire Gatinois in *Le Monde* on the same day: La Bourse est devenue un casino géant, selon les professionnels de la finance.

transactions accentuates this trend. Approximately 50% of stock exchange transactions in the USA and in Europe are conducted at a pace close to the speed of light. This computing power allows banks that can afford it and high-frequency traders to cancel in a microsecond, as is often the case, orders that they have just made at the same speed. The objective is to mislead the competitors who have also automated their financial transactions. The transmission of false information, before retracting it and attempting to take advantage of it, may prove to be profitable for the financial institution concerned, but such practices are in fact synonymous with a game of liar's poker rather than responsible investment.

Classic investors who do not have the means to use ultra-powerful computers to place their orders will lose out. In competition with much faster players than themselves, they will usually be disadvantaged. Each time they trade assets, they pay a kind of hidden commission imposed on them by high-frequency trading firms.[5] These firms take advantage of their clients. Their managers belong to the financial plutocracy and make off with a kind of right of passage, not on roads or bridges like in the Middle Ages, but rather on markets. The financial and IT experts they recruit act like mercenaries waging a financial war. They have to be the best in that headlong race against time that at the end of the day leads to nowhere. They always want to be the fastest, without ever wondering where they are going. High-frequency trading firms or big banks offer them golden bridges. What is the value of these "mercenaries" in the eyes of their employers?

Here, perhaps it is useful to make a parallel with the First World War. Within this framework, historian Niall Ferguson[6] addressed the issue of a soldier's value. He considers it to be the cost that his elimination by the enemy army represents. He pointed out that central powers were more effective in the fight than the allies. On average, it costs these powers $11,345 to kill an ally soldier, whereas the allies needed $36,485 to eliminate a German soldier. The latter therefore had close to three times more "value" than a British or French soldier. Similarly,

---

[5]See the book: *Flash Boys: A Wall Street Revolt* by Michael Lewis, published by W. W. Norton & Company in March 2014.

[6]The book is entitled: *The Pity of War*, author: Niall Ferguson, Allen Lane/Penguin Press, 1998.

the value of a "mercenary" who, in the current financial war, works for a high-frequency trading firm would be the significant cost that a competing business would have to pay in order to "beat" him in what would only be a microsecond, i.e. in order to be able to treat financial orders a microsecond before him. Therefore, in the eyes of their employers, these "mercenaries" are of great value. For the economy in general, they represent a cost, among others, through the hidden tax they have set up and through the erratic nature of the market prices they exacerbate.

At this point, it is worth mentioning that in 2015, $300 million was invested by the company Hibernia, in order to gain a handful of milliseconds for transactions between the two main financial centres, Wall Street and the City, an amount which would have been very useful, for example, in fighting child hunger. It shows that the priorities of our world have gone astray!

For stock markets, it is particularly profitable to allow their private clients, which are high-frequency trading companies, to use such technologies and thus take advantage of classical investors. Indeed, the commissions they receive are directly linked to the number of transactions. When they are conducted at high frequency, the profits collected by exchanges are therefore magnified.

Finally, the microsecond is tiny when compared to the temporal unit of business investments that require weeks, months and even years. The instant emerges from the electronic bets of casino finance that contradicts entrepreneurial needs.

Over-the-Counter Transactions

Most financial transactions are not conducted on organised markets but rather over-the-counter.[7] These are contracts between two financial players, the modalities of which are known only to them. Lack of transparency is the result, and in conjunction with the complexity of the financial system, it increases the risks of transmission of crises

---

[7]Over-the-counter (OTC) transactions are carried out directly between buyer and seller.

or financial shocks.[8] This situation allows systemic banks, involved in large-scale over-the-counter transactions, to keep their status and privileges and especially to continue to extract an economic rent or a guaranteed flow of income. In fact, the more a bank is susceptible of bringing down others in its fall, the more it increases its systemic nature, which allows it to benefit from a public guarantee financed by the taxpayer. Society is thus taken hostage.

Furthermore, in order to be operational, the invisible hand of Adam Smith obligatorily requires a market economy on which aggregate supply and demand intersect in such a way that prices and volumes can be set at equilibrium in a transparent manner. In addition to the lack of transparency, over-the-counter transactions are incompatible with the existence of such an economy.

As to derivatives often dealt with over the counter, the problem is more serious. Their prices mainly result from complex formulae or algorithms and therefore have only a remote connection to supply and demand.[9] With the development of over-the-counter transactions on derivatives, the risk is always less predictable and less measurable. It becomes opaque and diffuse, which has its effects on the economy and society.

Currencies are also essentially traded over-the-counter. FOREX is the most important financial market in the world, with average daily volumes of close to $5 trillion.

We are therefore faced with the paradox of an economy prone to entrepreneurial spirit and the risk-taking associated with it, and that at the same time has never issued so many derivatives or "hedging products" as now. These products are traded at such a scale that they generate a systemic risk for the global economy as well as for human society and nature.

---

[8]Organised markets with clearing houses should limit the transmission of financial shocks and should therefore play a buffer role.

[9]Obtaining derivatives prices is based on the unrealistic hypothesis of absence of arbitrage opportunities. But, the everyday operations of hedge funds and big banks consist precisely of taking advantage of such opportunities and creating them.

Bets in Casino Finance

The main function of derivatives is in reality to allow for large-scale bets within the framework of casino finance. There is no shortage of examples. Here are two.

The first concerns Credit Default Swaps (CDS) which are presented as a derivative product that allows its holder to insure himself or herself against the risk of a reference entity defaulting on payment. In essence, this means that a bank having lent a certain amount to a company and fearing that the debt will not be paid can, by buying CDSs, cover itself against such eventuality. In the event of payment default by the company, the bank triggers them, i.e. it contacts the financial institution from which it bought them so that it compensates its losses. Apparently, CDSs would be useful insurance contracts. However, in the specifications of these products a technical note often appears: it states it is not necessary to be exposed to the risk of the reference entity to buy them, which means that a bank can buy CDSs on a company,[10] even if it has not lent it any money. Why then should a bank need to hedge itself vis-à-vis a risk to which it is not subject? The answer is simple. In this case, it is not an insurance we are dealing with but a bet, a bet on the payment default or bankruptcy of the company concerned.[11] In everyday life, this is forbidden. No one can buy automobile insurance without owning a car. That would make no sense at all! No one is authorised to buy one or ten, even a hundred automobile insurance policies on their neighbour's car in the hope that he or she would have an accident, or having in mind the idea of sabotaging his car! Not only would that be immoral but completely senseless from an economic viewpoint and that is why such practices are forbidden in the case of cars. They are however allowed in the financial sector with CDSs.

---

[10]If the CDS is related to a country, European legislation apparently forbids this kind of practice. In fact, this regulation is very lax, as the most important players, i.e. in particular big banks, are exempt! This means that the great majority of these transactions are not concerned by this regulation!

[11]See also the scientific article: Endogenous Trading in Credit Default Swaps, Marc Chesney, Delia Coculescu and Selim Gokay, *Decisions in Economics and Finance*, Vol. 39, April 2016.

The second example considers life insurance policies which are turned into bets on death.[12] The myth recounts that Doctor Faust, by selling his soul to the devil, would have access to eternal youth. What would one think of those people who envisage increasing their wealth by betting on the death of their counterparts? Who have they sold their souls to? These questions are not only theoretical as today it is possible, thanks to a new avatar of financial innovation, to invest in life insurance policies that their holders wish to get rid of. In fact, in the USA they can resell their own insurance policy, known as life insurance, either to the insurance company that initially wrote it, which is still logical, or to a bank. In the latter case, who are the holders of life insurance policies that may be interested in such a sale? People of a certain age are particularly concerned: such an insurance policy for their children having become adults is no longer really necessary, and they may prefer to receive a lump sum that would be useful to them for other purposes. Sometimes, in a situation of financial distress, such a possibility can also help them pay possible debts or receive proper health care.

Which financial institutions are active in this field? Some major banks that purchase these contracts bundle and securitise[13] them after a diversification process. They then propose these products to investors. Diversifying risks means, for example, associating life insurance of individuals suffering from cancer with those of people with AIDS. As the reader will no doubt have understood, the risk that is being diversified is that of a death occurring too late. In fact, if individuals who sold their insurance are inconsiderate enough to prolong their existence beyond what is reasonable, investors will only receive the amount set out in the contract in a too distant future.

The payment that the bank will offer is related to the following factors: the actual age of such individual, his or her state of health and economic situation. This means that the older a person, the worse his or her health, and the more delicate his or her economic situation, the

---

[12]See: *Les contrats d'assurance vie qui se transforment en paris sur la mort*, Marc Chesney, Christine Hirszowicz and Brigitte Maranghino-Singer, in Der Schweizer Treuhänder, Vol. 10, 2010.

[13]Securitisation: process by which illiquid financial contracts are transformed into securities that are tradable on markets.

more interesting this person would be for the bank involved! The key variable in this calculation is therefore the mortality factor: the quicker death occurs, the more profitable this business is for the investor.

These two examples highlight the dangers that wagers of the casino finance represent. Those financial products that allow bets on the life of frail human beings or on bankruptcies of companies or countries are toxic from both a human and an economic point of view.

Misleading Structured Products

Structured products[14] are also bets of the casino finance. Their sale is particularly lucrative for large banks. For those clients that have purchased this type of product, there may be problems ahead.[15] The two examples below illustrate this.

Barrier Reverse Convertible (BRC)

This product is associated with an enhanced coupon, often 8% of the investment, i.e. CHF 8000 for an initial capital of CHF 100,000. The gains or losses in capital are determined by the prices of certain stocks, often three. If none of them goes below a certain barrier during a year, the holder of this product recovers their CHF 100,000. If one of the share prices falls and reaches a certain level, the so-called barrier, the holder will still obtain their CHF 8000 but will only receive a fraction of the capital invested, for example CHF 90,000 or 80,000. In other words, it is a complex, risky product as it is likely that at least one of the three prices will drop and the holder will not benefit from their eventual rise. Only the enhanced level of the coupon will partially compensate it. This product is similar to the junk bonds of the 1970s with a significant difference: its good rating. Indeed, contrary to the latter, this product receives

---

[14]**Structured products** most often result from the bundling of a number of derivatives. By nature, they are complex and difficult to understand for the client of a bank.

[15]At least 10% of global wealth is invested in this type of product.

very often A+ or AA from rating agencies, which can be misleading. In October 2013, Swiss bank Raiffeisen clients suffered significant losses with a financial product very similar to a BRC. These costs were the result of a drop of one of the shares (Zurich Insurance Group) making up the basket. This fall happened at the end of the last day of the reporting period and the value of the share fell precisely below the critical threshold. Clients who acquire these structured products also expose themselves to a risk of price manipulation inherent to this type of product.

Doublo, a Product Proposed by the Caisses d'Épargne in France

This time we are talking about a basket of twelve stocks. If in the space of six years, none of the 12 prices falls—which is very unrealistic—the capital will double. Otherwise, it would suffice for one of them to fall sufficiently during that period, which is highly probable, for the client to only recover its initial investment upon termination of the contract. The capital seems secure, and it is for this reason that this product is called "guaranteed capital" and is poorly regulated. In fact, the 267,000 investors who bought this product were also aggrieved.[16] No one saw their capital doubled, and because of the management fees imposed by the bank, after six years they recorded losses of between 2 and 6% of their investment: this means that they only received between €94,000 and 98,000 for an initial investment of €100,000. Therefore, it is a loss that was guaranteed for the client. Despite this, the Caisses d'Épargne sold this product in a life insurance format in 6 waves between 2001 and 2002 and succeeded in collecting an investment of around €2.1 billion. The French who bought it ended up having to bear the costs.

These two examples show how the client can be misled. With only a sketchy understanding of the concept of diversification, he may be led to believe that a greater number of stocks imply better diversification and therefore a safer investment. However, the exact opposite happens in this case as it is more likely that at least one of the stock prices will fall.

---

[16]See the link of the association fighting against bank abuses (CLAB): http://doublo.monde.free.fr/.

The one with the worst price dynamics has a determinant impact on the loss profile of this financial product. In 2016, structured products, the total of which in Europe reached approximately €600 billion,[17] and in 2017 in Switzerland, to CHF 275 billion,[18] represent a veritable danger for individuals, pension funds and municipalities. Paradoxically, governments condone this.

The Banking Sector Is Not Playing Its Role

The banking sector is not really performing its duties as the driving force of the economy. In 2012, in France, Germany and the UK, the amount that the banks allocated to loans for non-financial companies only corresponded to a small percentage of their balance sheet, 12, 18 and 5%,[19] respectively.

Many companies have difficulties obtaining loans from banks for their investments and that despite a policy of very low interest rates followed by the European Central Bank (ECB) in the hope of re-launching the economic machine. From the end of 2014, which marks the beginning of the ECB's quantitative easing policy, until the beginning of 2017, the volume of loans banks granted to companies only increased by 0.27% within the Eurozone, which is ridiculously weak.[20]

In December 2017, the interest rate on the main refinancing operations (MRO)[21] was kept null and the rate on the deposit facility, which is linked to the investments made by commercial banks on their account to the ECB, remained at a negative level: −0.4%. The leeway of the European Central Bank is now very limited. For companies,

---

[17]Source: *ESMA Report on Trends, Risks and Vulnerabilities*, No. 2, 2017. Europe is particularly active in terms of structured products.

[18]Source: SSPA Media, 30 January 2018.

[19]Liikanen, Erki, et al., *High-Level Expert Group on Reforming the Structure of the EU Banking Sector*, Brussels, 2012.

[20]Source: *Real Implications of Quantitative Easing in the Euro Area: A Complex-Network Perspective*, Chiara Perillo and Stefano Battiston, Working Paper, University of Zurich, 2018.

[21]The refinancing rate is the primary key interest rate of a central bank. It corresponds to the interest rate of the loans obtained by commercial banks from the central bank.

these financing difficulties are worrying in the sense that they limit the creation of new economic activities or the development of new technologies.

The banking sector is dominated by these institutions that are supposedly "too big to fail". In certain cases, the total on their balance sheet exceeds 100% of the GDP of the country where their headquarters are located, which is completely disproportionate. These banks are entirely oversized. Should they go bankrupt, the countries concerned would run considerable risks. In fact, in such a case, one would expect the State to bail out these institutions.

In 2017, the total balance sheet of UBS and Credit Suisse corresponded to 119% and 137% of the Swiss GDP,[22] respectively. HSBC, for example, was of the size of the British GDP. The balance sheets of the four largest French banks together, BNP Paribas, Société Générale, the BPCE group and Crédit Agricole, represented 317% of the corresponding GDP. In the case of Iceland, the three largest banks together represented 14 times the national GDP just before they went bankrupt in 2008!

In fact, these major banks are of an even more disproportionate size when all their activities, and not only those corresponding to their balance sheet, are taken into account. The "off-balance sheet"[23] is huge. It is close to a multiple of the balance sheet for large international banks, but is difficult to precisely gauge, as most often it is presented in an extremely opaque and complex manner. Its order of magnitude nevertheless may be established by considering the outstanding amount of derivatives of the banks under consideration. Indeed, these products most often appear off-balance sheet. In 2017, the nominal value of derivatives dealt with by Credit Suisse, meaning this bank's trading volume in terms of this type of financial products, was CHF 28.8 trillion

---

[22]Sources: UBS: *Annual Report* 2017, Zürich, p. 5 and Credit Suisse Group AG: *Annual Report* 2017, Zürich, Key metrics.

[23]**Off-balance sheet commitments** of a bank should correspond to those that, when in progress, have not yet generated the corresponding cash flows. It specifically concerns most derivatives-related activities. The exact definition of such commitments depends on the legal and regulatory framework considered.

and therefore corresponded to 36 times the total assets of the balance sheet and 687 times the total amount of shareholder equity of this bank, i.e. CHF 41.9 billion. Delusions of grandeur! This amount is also 43 times greater than the Swiss GDP, thus CHF 668.2 billion in 2017 and corresponding to 37.3% of global GDP.[24] Hedging activities, albeit economically viable, only represented less than 1% of this astronomical amount! The rest contributes to the development of casino finance.[25]

In 2017, the nominal value of derivatives dealt by UBS corresponded to CHF 18.5 trillion, i.e. 20 times its total balance sheet, 361 times its equity that totalled CHF 51.2 billion, and close to 28 times the Swiss GDP and 24% of world GDP.[26] Regarding HSBC, the nominal value of traded derivatives corresponded to 10.7 times total assets, 143 times equity, 11 times the British GDP and 33% of world GDP. In the case of Goldman Sachs, with $48.865 trillion, this volume represents 53.3 times total assets, 568.47 times equity or 2.52 times US GDP. For Citigroup, with $45.671 trillion, it represents 24.79 times total assets, 227.52 times equity or 2.36 times US GDP.

Regarding Deutsch Bank, in 2017 nominal value of derivatives represented close to €48.265 trillion,[27] i.e. 33 times its total balance sheet, 708 times its equity that totalled €68.1 billion, 15 times the German GDP or approximately two-thirds of global GDP!

Who still thinks the situation is under control?

Furthermore, the obligation imposed on taxpayers to bail out major banks in a tricky situation only worsens the problem. Indeed, their management are encouraged to engage even more in risky activities as they expect these banks to benefit from a free default insurance. This results in an increase in their off-balance sheet size.

---

[24]Source: Credit Suisse Group AG: *Annual Report* 2017, p. 325, Zürich.

[25]In the case of Lehman Brothers just before it declared bankruptcy in September 2008, the nominal value of derivatives corresponded to approximately 50 times the total balance sheet and 1500 times shareholder equity! See: *The Failure Resolution of Lehman Brothers*, p. 142, Federal Reserve Bank of New York, Michael J. Fleming and Asani Sarkar, December 2014, as well as: Lehman Brothers, *Annual Report* 2007.

[26]Source: UBS: *Annual Report* 2017, Zürich, p. 363.

[27]See: *Annual Report*, Deutsche Bank, 2017, Frankfurt, pp. 28 and 109.

Moreover, besides the implicit or even explicit public guarantee given to them, these so-called too big to fail institutions are financed at interest rates lower than those of the market. As they are presumed to not be exposed to the risk of bankruptcy, they appear more attractive in the eyes of investors and therefore benefit from subsidies that total billions of euros. For the period between 2011 and 2012, these subsidies for the big banks represented, according to the IMF,[28] close to $50 billion in the USA, just as in Switzerland, i.e. on average $25 billion a year. For Switzerland, this amount is in contrast to, on the one hand, the contribution of the finance sector to the gross national product that was assessed at CHF 36 billion for the year 2013[29] and on the other hand to lower subsidies of about CHF 3.5 billion a year, allocated to agriculture during this same period. In Japan and in the UK, the subsidies the big banks received would be around $110 billion and, in the European Union, it would reach $300 billion during the same period of time.

In addition to their too big to fail status, they have at least two other advantages: firstly, the possibility to use their off-balance sheet assets, already mentioned above, for highly speculative deals, and secondly, to create a bad bank[30] if the risks get too high. What other sector of activity has so many advantages? Not the craft sector, nor agriculture, nor industry! Let's imagine a baker, a restaurateur, a watchmaking or IT company being able on the one hand to camouflage outside of the balance sheet any potentially risky or dubious activities and on the other to create a "bad bakery" or a "bad restaurant", a "bad watchmaking or IT company" to avoid possible insolvability at taxpayers' expense? No, not for a second! And how many big banks would already be bankrupt

---

[28]International Monetary Fund, *Global Financial Stability Report, Moving from Liquidity- to Growth-Driven Markets*, April 2014, Washington, DC, p. 114.

[29]This value creation of the financial sector dropped to reach CHF32 billion in 2015. See: Pharmafirmen schlagen Banken, Birgit Volgt, *NZZ am Sonntag*, 29 January 2017.

[30]A Bad Bank's task consists in taking charge and then liquidating the bad assets of the bank that created them. If this bank is unfortunately too big to fail, the taxpayers will very often take it upon themselves to dispose of the waste and as a last resort bail it out.

without these multiple privileges? In Italy, the banking sector situation is particularly critical because in 2016 it was crippled with approximately €200 billion of bad debt.

The possibility of deducting their penalties from their taxes, albeit partially, represents a supplementary gift offered to the big banks.[31] For example, this happened with Credit Suisse in the case of the CHF 2.9 billion fine imposed on it by a US court in 2014.

Banca della Svizzera Italiana (BSI) allowed thousands of very wealthy American clients to avoid taxes, thanks to the use of tax havens and financial arrangements of all types, and wanted to deduct from its taxes a part of the $211 million fine it had to pay to the USA in 2015.[32] None of this prevented it from disappearing following serious misappropriation. The Federal Financial Market Supervisory Authority (FINMA) withdrew its banking licence in 2016 at a time when it was being taken over by EFG bank.

A tax deduction of €1.7 billion had already been granted to Société Générale in 2008, following the Kerviel affair mentioned in the first chapter.

Such deductions constitute unjustifiable privileges. Drivers are not allowed to reduce fines in the same way!

These privileges can only contribute to the increase in power of the financial sector in the economy. A study shows that 147 companies controlled close to 40% of the global economy in 2007. Some 98% of the first 50 companies belong to the financial sector. A large part of them, too big to fail, benefitted from state financial support.[33]

---

[31]The Swiss Federal Court decided in late October 2016 that this privilege should disappear. Cf. Unternehmen können Bussen steuerlich nicht absetzen, *NZZ*, 12 October 2016.

[32]See article in the *NZZ am Sonntag* of 5 April 2015: Bank BSI muss Busse von 211 Millionen innert sieben Tagen an die USA bezahlen.

[33]Vitali, Stefania, Glattfelder, James B., and Battiston, Stefano, The Network of Global Corporate Control, *PLoS One*, Vol. 6, No. 10, 2011.

The Tricks of Stress Tests

The purpose of stress tests is to check the resilience of the banking sector. They generally focus on two types of scenarios: a standard and a critical one. However, these tests are problematic as none of them conducted before the critical phases of the crisis generated an alert signal.

A remarkable example is that of Iceland where such tests were conducted in August 2008 in the four principal banks in the country. Their conclusions were very reassuring. As Jonas Jonsson, director of Iceland's Financial Supervisory Authority stated, "The results of the stress tests indicate that the financial ratios of the banks are solid and they can resist considerable financial shocks". In fact, after manipulation of the stock prices and misappropriations of all types,[34] the three most important banks declared bankruptcy on 6, 7 and 9 October 2008 and ended up being nationalised.

The same thing happened in Ireland where the three most important banks (Allied Irish, Anglo Irish and National Irish) were submitted to stress tests and successfully passed them. The reassuring results divulged in July 2010 forecasted a healthy financial situation. In fact, this was not the case. In November of the same year, these three banks saw their depositors flee and found themselves, especially Allied Irish Bank, in a critical situation of virtual bankruptcy. The establishment of a bailout plan thought up by the European Union, the European Central Bank and the IMF helped prevent this from happening.

---

[34]Cf. Iceland to Sentence Ninth Banker Found Guilty of Market Manipulation That Helped Caused 2008 Crash, *Independent,* 7 October 2016, as well as: How Big Was the Fall of the Banks in an International Context? *Morgunblaðið* (Iceland's oldest newspaper), Jared Bibler, 11 March 2010 and finally: *When Kaupthing Tried to Move Its CDS (in 2008) with a Little Help from a Friend,* in link: http://uti.is/2015/12/when-kaupthing-tried-to-move-its-cds-in-2008-with-a-little-help-from-a-friend/ posted by Sigrún Davídsdóttir, 8 December 2015. According to these sources, the Kaupthing Bank manipulated its stock prices by way of a large scale and fraudulent repurchase of its own shares. It also tried to manipulate the price of its CDS (defined above in this chapter) by arranging with the Deutsche Bank for it to issue huge volumes in the hope of bringing down their price.

In the Spring of 2009, stress tests were conducted in the USA. They were affected by a bias as their hypotheses were prepared in such a way that even in the so-called unfavourable scenario they would not generate catastrophic consequences. Otherwise, if the results indicated that the financial system ran the risk of sinking, the effect could have been devastating and would have only hurried things along. It would have run that risk even more quickly. The hypotheses of the models used for the stress tests were such that the results, pointing the way to possible shortcomings in the system, are global bearers of hope to the extent that these problems must appear to have a solution. The hypotheses contribute to forge reality. That the model's conclusions confirm the hopes of recovery and the latter will be sustained even if only on the short term; that they dismiss them and the imbalances might worsen.

According to a document from the Board of Governors of the Federal Reserve System,[35] the unfavourable scenario must "reflect serious but also plausible conditions". This means that, according to that institution co-responsible for the implementation of stress tests, a catastrophic scenario is by design not plausible! How can one take the financial system stress tests seriously when the possibility of serious shocks is excluded?

As far as the evaluation of the 19 banks affected by the tests is concerned, artificially overvalued toxic financial assets as well as the transfer of bad assets in off-balance-sheet structures were sufficient to guarantee reassuring results.

The results of these highly political tests corresponded perfectly to the hypotheses used and were in line with the messages that the administration wished to send with the aim of restoring market confidence. According to Timothy Geithner, then Treasury Secretary, none of the biggest 19 American banks presented a risk of insolvability. For Ben Bernanke, President of the Federal Reserve during these tests, these results should comfort investors and American citizens. The implicit message was that, in case of serious financial problems for these banks, the State, meaning the taxpayer, would bail them out.

---

[35]See the report entitled: *The Supervisory Capital Assessment Program: Design and Implementation*, 24 April 2009, p. 5.

Similar stress tests were conducted in 2010 in Europe. Their results were divulged in July of that year. According to the Bank of France and the Prudential Supervisory Authority,[36] "the adverse scenario, already extremely pessimistic, was aggravated with the very harsh hypotheses of a shock on the sovereign exposures held in the trading portfolio of the banks and the loans to the private sector recorded in the banking book…". A short time after the publication of the results this "adverse, extremely pessimistic" and even "aggravated" scenario was already reality for a certain number of European countries, and precisely because these tests excluded the possibility of sovereign defaults. This means that they did not consider that the integration of banks' losses in public accounts could lead European States to insolvability.

One wonders how the tests regarding the solidity of the financial situation of the banks could suppose that even in the worst case scenario, the financial situation of countries such as Greece, Portugal, Italy, Ireland or Spain would be under control! With such hypotheses, it is not surprising that the conclusions were reassuring!

In 2011, new stress tests were conducted in Europe. Their hypotheses basically corresponded to those of 2010 and even excluded that a European country, by chance Greece, could default. In August 2011, shortly after the announcement of reassuring results concerning the financial health of the banks, renewed turbulances came to shake Europe, and the allegedly solid banks saw their share prices plunge! *Société Générale* stock lost 27% during the first two weeks of the month. Between 1 July and 12 September 2011, the three most important French banks, BNP Paribas, Crédit Agricole and Société Générale, lost over 50% of their market capitalisation.

Likewise in October 2014, the European Central Bank presented the results of the most recent stress tests conducted in Europe. The purpose of the tests was to analyse the situation of 130 banks on 31 December 2013.

---

[36]Press release from the Bank of France and the Prudential Supervisory Authority dated 23 July 2010. Results of the European stress test: *French Banks Among the Most Solid in Europe.*

On that date, according to the results, 25 of them would have failed. Between the end of December 2013 and end of October 2014, twelve of these would however have improved their financial situation by way of recapitalisations. Apparently, only thirteen banks continued to be fragile and needed to increase their equity.

Therefore, in the end, 90% of the institutions finally passed the tests successfully! 13 banks, i.e. 10% failed. This percentage is politically correct. Two or three per cent failure would have led one to think that the procedure was too lax. Conversely, 20% failure would have been perceived as a worrying sign of fragility of the banking sector. The content of this list is also politically correct. In fact, the big German or French banks were not part of it. How fortunate that the enormous fine of approximately \$8.8 billion that BNP Paribas had to pay the USA concerns a period after 31 December 2013!

However, these tests allegedly stricter than the previous ones have an optimistic unfavourable scenario. The risk of deflation of the Eurozone was in fact excluded, as was the risk of a European country defaulting. And in the worst case scenario, unemployment in 2016 would only have been 21.6% in Greece. This scenario should have corresponded to the favourable case as in that country unemployment was 24.9 and 23.1% in the first and second quarters of 2016, respectively.

Among the banks assessed, 76 had under 5% equity as a percentage of the total of their respective total assets. Among them, 20 were German, especially Deutsche Bank, 10 French, with the national champions BNP Paribas, Crédit Agricole, the only agricultural thing about it being its name, and Société Générale, and 10 were Spanish and 10 Italian. A bank with less than 5% equity on its balance sheet becomes insolvent when its losses, linked, for example, to the drop in the prices of its assets or to significant fines, exceed this small percentage.[37] Such losses are possible and could result in a cascade of bankruptcies, given the financial links that unite these banks. It appears therefore that the results of these stress tests and those ran subsequently do not stand up to the scrutiny of the situation.

---

[37]See: Secteur bancaire: Tout va très bien, madame la Marquise, *Le Monde*, 28 October 2014 à 11h53, Jézabel Couppey-Soubeyran.

Generally speaking, the results of these exercises regarding financial solidity, which should be reassuring, and their publication, often shortly before a coming financial disturbance, illustrate the inability of most of the models used in the tests to really understand the risky nature of the sector of systemic banks, and to face the facts: their so-called profitability is mainly due to the ongoing public financial support and guaranties of all sorts they receive. They are too often tests of convenience that turn out to be a farce. Who can still believe that, despite the huge amount of public funds swallowed up by the banking system, it is on the road to becoming stable and that the situation is under control?

Rating Agencies and the Conflict of Interest

In a market economy with efficient and transparent financial markets, rating agencies should only play a limited role. Bond prices should in fact reflect all pertinent information, and ratings should be superfluous. The mere existence of these agencies and the role given them show how dysfunctional the current so-called market economy is.

Historically, these agencies were created in the late nineteenth and early twentieth century to allow investors to better understand the risk and profits associated with the new technologies of the time, such as the railway. Today, instead of concentrating on new technologies, such as the Internet, and on the quality of their shares or bonds, i.e. on the risk associated with this sector, they generally study the quality of the bonds, issued by both the public and private sectors. This leads to two comments. On the one hand, a serious analysis of the IT sector would have been particularly useful as it would have helped prevent the Internet bubble in 2001 or at least limit it; instead of that, the agencies discredited themselves before the financial crisis by giving the best ratings to the worst of the financial debt products. On the other hand, the transformation process of simple debts in financial securities is decisive and of a complexity that is totally out of proportion. The big banks create special purpose vehicles, meaning ad hoc entities, to which they resell a number of their loans. By alleviating their balance sheet in this way, they are removing a credit risk they consider excessive. Within the framework of these funds, these loans are bundled and transformed into financial securities[38] which are then sold to investors who are sufficiently naïve to believe that a good rating means quality. Therefore, by producing special purpose vehicles and financial assets, big banks considerably increase the complexity of the financial sector and implicitly justify the existence of rating agencies.

It should also be noted that the ratings issued by these agencies also serve as means of pressure on countries to implement measures favourable to the financial sector. By not doing so, the forecasts associated with these ratings run the risks of being fulfilled, meaning that these agencies are so powerful that their prophecies can come true.

Certain companies can also be under pressure. The case of the reinsurer Hannover Re illustrates this problem. In the late 1990s, this company had contracts with the rating agencies Standard & Poor's and A. M. Best. Moody's also wanted to strike a deal. Hannover Re refused its offer, which did not prevent Moody's from assessing this company over the following three years. It gave it ratings always lower than those issued by Standard & Poor's, in the hope of finally getting such a contract. This drop in their rating placed the board and shareholders under pressure as it resulted in a drop of 10% of their share price.[39]

Finally, it should be emphasised that big banks and hedge funds are shareholders and important clients of rating agencies. This creates significant conflict of interests incompatible both with well-functioning financial markets and with the principals of a liberal economy. These conflict of interests question the objectivity and the seriousness of these rating systems since according to different sources the establishment of a rating only requires on average two or three hours of work.[40]

---

[38]The loans are thus "securitised", i.e., they have been transformed into financial securities tradable on the markets. See in this chapter, the second example of bets of casino finance.

[39]See Rügemer, Werner, *Rating-Agenturen, Einblicke in die Kapitalmacht der Gegenwart*, Bielefeld, Transcript Verlag, 2012, p. 93 and Credit Rater's Power Leads to Abuses, Some Borrowers Says, in *Washington Post*, 24 November 2004.

[40]Ibid., the above-mentioned book.

Manipulation of Interest Rates

London Interbank Offered Rate (Libor) is the international reference of financial contracts, the total amount of which reaches close to $350 trillion.[41] This means that it is essential for international finance to operate. It is often used when individuals get into debt to buy apartments or cars. In a market economy, its determination should come from a market mechanism. This is not the case.

It is not market transactions that establish it but rather unverifiable information. For 5 currencies, 8–16 banks indicate the rate at which they refinance themselves, at 11 a.m. London time, and this covers 7 different maturities. Libor results from the average of this, the lowest and highest levels of which are excluded.

In 2007, when interbank lending became almost non-existent, at the end of the day Libor was primarily based on such unverifiable information.

This manipulation can be explained in two ways. On the one hand, it helps optimise gains on derivatives, in particular those attached to interest rates,[42] often linked to Libor. On the other hand, to announce a lower financing rate allows banks to claim good solvability and therefore try to improve its reputation.

According to a Financial Services Authority in London report, between 2005 and 2008 Barclays bank made at least 257 attempts to manipulate the US Dollar Libor, the Yen Libor and Euribor.[43]

As far as UBS is concerned, between 2005 and 2010, over 1000 attempts of manipulation were counted and involved over 30 people in different services or countries. Certain members of the management board may even have encouraged such operations.[44]

---

[41]See: *Libor's Rise Matters for Trillions of Debt*, Liz McCormick, Bloomberg, 13 Decmeber 2017.

[42]These are derivatives, defined in Chapter 2, but associated to an interest rate and not for example to a stock.

[43]Hosp, Gerald, Vom Referenzzinssatz zum Skandalwert, *NZZ*, 20 December 2012, p. 27.

[44]Schöchli, Hansueli, Hohe Hürden für Strafbehörden im Libor-Fall, *NZZ*, 24 January 2013, p. 9.

UBS paid external traders £15,000 per quarter to help it coordinate manipulations with other banks. In fact, these wrongdoings require a certain cooperation[45]: on its own, a bank could never accomplish its aims as Libor results from an average of inputs provided by different banks. There are in fact about twelve which have been suspected of attempts at manipulations.

UBS had to pay American, English and Swiss regulatory authorities a fine in the amount of $1.4 billion, i.e. three times more than Barclays.

In December 2013, UBS escaped a fine of €2.5 billion from the European Commission. Revealing its fraud to that institution allowed it to obtain full immunity. Committing fraud, then if necessary, reporting its own wrongdoings and that of its competitors quickly, before other institutions involved do so, appears to be a winning strategy for big banks. This helps generate important gains if the fraud is not detected and should it be detected, to avoid the penalties.

Within the framework of this scandal, UBS nevertheless had to pay other bills. According to the *NZZ*, it spent close to CHF 100 million on costs associated with internal analysis and the monitoring of millions of data. These tasks required among other things the involvement of 410 lawyers.[46]

Société Générale and Deutsche Bank were also involved in these manipulations, with the latter having to pay a penalty of $2.5 billion.[47] Since the onset of the scandal, several banks have had to pay fines totalling $7 billion, whereas the profits generated by these tricks have amounted to approximately $23 billion. The overall bill and sentences delivered are very limited!

The competent authorities probably wished to limit the scale of the scandal out of fear of increasing what they probably perceived as a systemic risk. "Too big to fail" was thus accompanied with "too big to jail", i.e. a refusal to hand out jail sentences to the board of the banks involved in these questionable practices.

---

[45]Bräuer, Sebastian, and Hug, Daniel, UBS in Konflikt mit Aktionären, *NZZ am Sonntag*, 23 December 2012.

[46]Ibid.

[47]Deutsche Bank is expected to pay a fine of $70 million in the USA for its 2007–2012 manipulation of the ISDAFIX, a rate used for derivative contracts.

A section on the manipulation of interest rates should also mention the monetary policy followed by most central banks, analysed in chapter two, and that consisted in, among other things, buying astronomical amounts of bonds, most often coming from so-called sovereign States. Negative interest rates are the result of this policy. In July 2016, about one-third of the public debt of developed countries, and 60% in the case of Germany had negative returns. On a global scale in 2017, the value of bonds with negative returns was $9.000 trillion.[48] This means that this phenomenon is far from negligible. It should be recalled that the interest rate is the price of money. If a price is negative and remains so for some time, it can only result from large-scale manipulation of the market considered, here the bond market. And central banks are the true players. When interest rates finally bounce back, the losses could be in trillions of dollars for bond holders.[49]

Manipulation of Exchange Rates

Just like Libor, the foreign exchange market was also manipulated. It would have been surprising if it hadn't! These misappropriations were carried out between 2008 and 2013 and were made public in 2014. Six major banks were involved in these manipulations: Bank of America, Citibank, HSBC, JP Morgan Chase, Royal Bank of Scotland and UBS.

The latter had to pay the biggest amount: a total of approximately CHF 774 million to the competent authorities in the USA, England and Switzerland. This concerned fines or the restitution of profits linked to these misappropriations. In the case of Switzerland, UBS had to pay CHF 134 million, an amount corresponding only to the earnings generated by these manipulation and which is therefore not really a fine. This is a perfect situation for UBS. If misappropriations are not detected, earnings are realised. Otherwise, they are reimbursed. It is as if one would be satisfied to ask a thief to return the goods he had stolen. That would only encourage him to do it all over again.

---

[48]See: Over $9tn of Bonds Trade with Negative Yields Article, *Financial Times* of 17 August 2017.
[49]See: Toxische Verschuldung, Andreas Uhlig, *NZZ*, 31 October 2016.

UBS has a commission responsible for managing risks and their potential effects in terms of reputation loss. The members of this commission were outrageously paid: at least CHF 500,000 a year. They clearly did not treat this case of exchange rate manipulations with the attention it deserved. If it is confirmed that this bank will not pay a fine in Switzerland, the country where its main headquarters are located, these risks are limited and one can understand why this commission must have had other priorities.

The show goes on. According to the *Financial Times*,[50] "Eight of the world's largest banks are set to discuss financial settlements with the European Commission, drawing a line under a four-year probe into allegations they formed a cartel to rig the $5.3tn global foreign exchange market".

To conclude this chapter, it should be recalled that the market is central to a liberal argument. It must, by way of the mechanism-forming process, organise the economy in an effective manner. As far as financial markets are concerned, now the nervous system of the economy, this mechanism is currently defect.

Within the context of the current casino finance, in which powerful players are in a position to influence or manipulate stock prices and are thus associated with numerous scandals and offences, market prices do not truly represent the fundamental values of the assets.

Financial markets are no longer able to play the role they are supposed to, which consists of allowing an optimal allocation of capital and risks. When the capital is used for bets rather than for investments, it loses its productive nature and therefore their nature as capital.

The financial sector has become foreign to the entrepreneurial spirit. The financialisation of the economy contradicts the basic principles of liberalism on which this sector is supposed to be based. In the financial sphere, the invisible hand of Adam Smith is less and less operative to the extent that seeking to meet individual interests generates a systemic risk and therefore harms the general welfare. It is often replaced by the hand of the casino finance croupier who collects the winnings for the so-called systemic banks and hedge funds.

---

[50]*Financial Times*, Banks Prepare to Settle with Brussel over Forex Cartel Probe, 19 November 2017.

Bibliography

Credit Suisse Group AG: *Annual Report*, Zurich, 2017.

Deutsche Bank, *Annual Report*, Frankfurt, 2017.

Ferguson, Niall, *The Pity of War*, Allen Lane/Penguin Press, 1998.

Financial Times, Banks Prepare to Settle with Brussel over Forex Cartel Probe, 19 November 2017.

Fleming, Michael J., and Sarkar, Asani, *The Failure Resolution of Lehman Brothers*, Federal Reserve Bank of New York, December 2014.

International Monetary Fund, *Global Financial Stability Report, Moving from Liquidity- to Growth-Driven Markets*, April 2014, Washington, DC.

Keynes, John Maynard, *The General Theory of Employment, Interest and Money*, Macmillan Cambridge University Press, 1936.

Lehman Brothers, *Annual Report*, 2007.

Lewis, Michael, *Flash Boys: A Wall Street Revolt*, W. W. Norton & Company, 2014.

McCormick, Liz, *Libor's Rise Matters for Trillions of Debt*, Bloomberg, 13 Decmeber 2017.

Over $9tn of Bonds Trade with Negative Yields Article, *Financial Times*, 17 August 2017.

Rügemer, Werner, *Rating-Agenturen, Einblicke in die Kapitalmacht der Gegenwart*, Bielefeld, Transcript Verlag, 2012.

UBS *Annual Report*, Zurich, 2017.

5

The Birth of Homo-Financiarius and the Subservience of the Elite

And during this time, what are the political and economic elites doing? They are busy, most often beating about the bush on television programmes. They don't seem to be too concerned about the system's collapse and many of them are even spreading the idea that the crisis is over.

Isn't the best way to solve a problem to deny its existence? The page would have already been turned and proof would have been given by recent bull markets. This phenomenon, mainly due to unprecedented liquidity injections by central banks and a massive indebtedness, merely reflects the growing disconnection between the financial sector and the economy, discussed in chapter two. As to this regard, it should be added that since the onset of the crisis, a number of them, the Swiss National Bank in particular, have acquired colossal amounts of stock, which keeps financial markets on life support.

And meanwhile, the academic world just purrs with satisfaction. Its numerous circles of economists hover around the power. To become "the Prince's adviser" is the ultimate aim of most of its members. Moreover, big banks increasingly fund university chairs and thus

© The Author(s) 2018
M. Chesney, *A Permanent Crisis*,
https://doi.org/10.1007/978-3-030-00518-4_5

have influence over those benefiting from such funds as well as indirectly over education and research. These same financial institutions, bailed out by public funds to avoid bankruptcy, spread the gospel and subsidise professors or possibly students by offering them awards. They also give donations to organise economics or finance conferences. All of this actually represents a hidden cost for the academic world. On the one hand, the latter is in fact complicit in institutions' attempts to clear their dubious reputations associated with numerous scandals. On the other hand, it promotes the Chicago School which defends unbridled deregulation of markets supposedly resulting in an effective economic system and a natural hierarchy of winners and losers. As analysed in the preceding chapter, this dubious recipe in fact leads to casino finance with disastrous social consequences. This school of thought, comforted in its monopoly of ideas and economic concepts in the academic world, exercises veritable influence on most of the circles of economists and governments. The few economists who dare to question this school are in fact marginalised.

For some members of these circles, a crisis would have positive effects linked to the process of "creative destruction" (sic!) which despite destroying jobs, should also create new ones. If the destruction process really works, its desired effect is less perceptible. At the international level, around 30 million jobs have in fact been destroyed with the crisis but the massive creation of new jobs, due to the emergence of new technologies or new means of production, has not been a tangible reality!

This theory recalls the opinions in vogue in certain milieus before the First World War and at the time of its outbreak.[1] If a crisis can trigger "creative destruction", a war, especially that of 1914–1918, would have a "cleansing" effect. If these catastrophes constitute kinds of unavoidable cyclical purges, they would be part of the nature of things and therefore

---

[1] A reference work on the topic of war and modernity from the late nineteenth century to 1914 is the work written by Emilio Gentile, *L'apocalisse della modernità. La Grande Guerra per l'uomo nuovo*, Mondadori, Milan, 2008.

could generate positive effects. Heinrich Mann explained that "some, not to say most, had had more than enough of it" and that they perceived the First World War as a kind of "promise of renewal".[2]

Well before the war of 1914–1918, Dostoyevsky declared in 1877 in *A Writer's Diary*:

> It is obvious that war also serves a purpose, it is salubrious, it comforts mankind. It is indignant if we look at it abstractly [far from its concrete reality] but in practice it appears to work exactly because for a contaminated body even something as beneficial as peace becomes an annoyance[3]

Just as revealing is what Nietzsche wrote in *Thus Spoke Zarathustra* in 1883:

> You shall love peace as a means to new wars, and the short peace more than the long one!'… War and courage have done more great things than love of one's neighbor.[4]

Or, when in *Human, All Too Human* in 1878, Nietzsche wrote that from a war "mankind emerges from it stronger for good and for evil".[5] These proposals contrast with those of the writer Blaise Cendrars who having taken part in the First World War wrote in his work *La Main coupée* (The Severed Hand):

> It is a fine thing to die for one's country…" is that not true? Do you think you are at the theatre [Théâtre de la Comédie Française, *NDT*], Sir? Have you lost your sense of reality? Have you any idea about what is hidden behind that alexandrine verse? War is ignominious. At most this

---

[2]Mann, Heinrich, *Die Verräter, Sämtliche Erzählungen* III, S. Fischer, 1996, p. 516: «Manche, wenn nicht die meisten, hatten irgendetwas gründlich satt» and «Der Krieg versprach eine Erfrischung».

[3]Dostoïevski, Fiodor, *A Writer's Diary*, Northwestern Univesity Press, USA, 2009, Own Translation.

[4]Nietzsche, Friedrich, *Thus Spoke Zarathustra*, Cambridge University Press, USA, 2006, pp. 199 and 33 respectively.

[5]Nietzsche, Friedrich, *Human, All Too Human*, Cambridge University Press, UK, 1986, p. 163

spectacle can satisfy the eyes or the heart of a cynical philosopher and address the logic of the darkest pessimism. A dangerous life may suit an individual, yes, but on a social level it leads directly to tyranny, especially in a republic led by a senate of elderly men, a chamber of chatter-mongers, an academy of did-you-see-me, a school of generals...[6]

The First World War and those following it in the twentieth century have not resulted in the appearance of that superman, so dear to Nietzsche, the *subject* of destiny and History, but rather they have seen the rise in power of the pale figure of the uneducated homo economicus, who optimises his gains and therefore who is himself determined and *object*.

With neoliberalism's seize of power in the 1980s, this creature has changed and has mutated into homo-financiarius, a predatory creature, harmful to society, characterised by a profound cynicism with a tendency to senselessly accumulate wealth. The superman should make it possible to go beyond the Judeo-Christian system of values, the homo-financiarius represents a regression in relation to these values; his are purely financial and he is ready to do anything to meet them. Max Weber analysed the protestant religion's importance in the development of capitalism. Today the Temple merchants and the golden calf worshippers are in power. They are the high priests of casino finance, of a rogue religion where cynicism in its pure state is the required quality. Didn't Lloyd Craig Blankfein, Chairman and CEO of Goldman Sachs and false prophet before the Lord, state in 2009 that he was "doing God's work"! Financial markets are the God of this new religion. The homo-financiarius adores and fears them at the same time. Money is its idol and his fetish. His places of worship are the casino finance trading rooms; its heaven is the instant of eternity provided by unlimited bonuses. Its most important myth is that of the invisible hand, referred to above, focusing on the ideal functioning of the markets. Its language is often complicated, dressed up in scientific clothing that impresses believers more than it convinces them. Like Latin, for the Roman

---

[6]Cendrars, Blaise, *La Main coupée (1946)*, Gallimard, Folio, Paris, 2002, p. 378, Own Translation.

Catholic Church before the Second Vatican Council, this hermetic language is reserved for the initiated. It allows for the creation of a ritual, a communication based on a mysterious support undecipherable for the common mortal. As to the sale of indulgences, it has now been resuscitated, albeit under a new form. The state is expected to spend enormous amounts of money to finance the bailout and subsidies of financial mastodons in the hope that financial markets will prove to be lenient with them in order to facilitate obtaining future loans. This development is detrimental to society.

The key growth factors of the financialised economy, far from savings and investment, the true development of which is due, according to Max Weber, to the emergence of Protestantism, have turned into debts and dubious bets, often at the expense of society.

If the financialised economy has become a rogue religion, if financial bankruptcy is no more than the result of moral bankruptcy then a new Reformation is necessary: a reformation of a special type, as it is not about creating a new religion but rather putting people and the planet in the centre of the economy. This reformation should first of all address the question of society's values and those of the individuals in it, bringing to light the fact that the true values of our society should not be financial and that *being* should not be mixed up with *having*. This question falls outside a strictly economic framework, it is of a philosophical, religious and political nature. What is at stake is putting finance in its place at the service of the economy and putting the economy at the service of society.

The Subservience of the Elite

In his 1927 book, *The Treason of the Intellectuals*,[7] Julien Benda analysed how at the time the intellectual elites betrayed their mission by adopting, on behalf of pragmatism, xenophobic and ultra-nationalist stances instead of promoting the spirit of the Enlightenment thus serving and defending these "eternal and altruistic values" that are the values of the spirit.

---

[7]Benda, Julien, *The Treason of the Intellectuals*, Taylor and Francis, USA, 2007.

It is also a betrayal by the elite that we witness today, not like in the period between the two world wars, and of the Fascist or Stalinist dictatorships' rise to power in Europe, but by way of the neoliberal seizing of power, explicitly or implicitly supported by most of the elite.

Moral bankruptcy, linked to the subservience of the elites, is of a different nature from that of a company or a country. It is disastrous as it ruins the values on which our society is allegedly based. Savings, trust and responsibility are supplanted, in the centre of the financial system, by indebtedness, cynicism and the socialisation of losses. As far as non-monetizable values are concerned, the most important ones, such as honesty, integrity, friendship and honour, tend to be obliterated, relegated to the antique shop.

This moral bankruptcy, this intellectual corruption of the elites, or of those who pretend to be, is associated with a confusion of ideas and concepts. To return to the theses of Francis Fukuyama, after the fall of the Berlin wall, liberalism and democracy, are supposed to constitute the ultimate phase of capitalism towards which human society had been converging over the last centuries. In the name of realism, this vision imposed itself among the "elites". Paradoxically, this presumed unsurpassable state of equilibrium supposed to characterise today's society suffers from serious imbalances. How can such a state be compatible with the present situation characterised by casino finance, by an impoverishment and weakening of entire segments of the population and by a democracy that is more virtual than real?

The higher education system has a responsibility in this process of converting the future elite to realism. As mentioned in an appeal published in 2011,[8] "More than three years since the outbreak of the financial and macroeconomic crisis that highlighted the pitfalls, limitations, dangers and responsibilities of main-stream thought in economics, finance and management, the quasi-monopolistic position of such thought within the academic world nevertheless remains largely unchallenged". Instead

---

[8]Appeal of teachers and researchers: *Renewing the Research and Teaching in Finance, Economics and Management to Better Serve the Common Good*, Genève-Fribourg-Zürich March 2011, online: http://www.responsiblefinance.ch/appeal/.

of contributing to the common good, the research very often produces "complacent analysis about the supposed benefits that the economic system may derive from the financialization of economic and social activities driven by the alleged benefits of financial innovation and speculation".

Counterfeit Intellectual Money

Putting on a pedestal alleged experts who occupy important positions without enough scientific or democratic control magnifies this conversion of intellectual elites to realism and therefore ultimately their betrayal. The nomination of the Nobel Prizes in Economics (or more precisely of the Prizes of the central bank of Sweden in Economic Sciences in memory of Alfred Nobel[9]) illustrates this issue. With great media coverage and excessively praised, they are in a position to influence governments on their economic policies, companies on their investment policies and academic institutions on their teaching and research strategies. Jean Tirole recipient of this prize in 2014 wrote, after his nomination, to the Minister of Higher Education and Research in France to block any attempt to introduce pluralism in the field of economics. This correspondence bore fruit as no new academic fields were created, which allows the monolithic way of thinking in that country to keep its power within the academic world.

It should be noted, moreover, that numerous so-called Nobel prize winners are linked to the University of Chicago's school of thought known for promoting as much market deregulation as possible—this being, however, one of the causes of the crisis—and that two of them, Robert Merton and Myron Scholes, having received the prize in 1997, were subsequently associated with the LTCM investment fund and its

---

[9]In December 2004, Peter Nobel, Alfred's descendant, declared in an interview: "*Nowhere in Alfred Nobel's correspondence can one find the least mention of a prize in economics. The Royal Bank of Sweden placed its egg in another bird's very respectable nest and thus infringes on the Nobel "registered trademark"*".

quasi-bankruptcy in 1998.[10] The dominance of this school of thought was also illustrated in 2013, with two of the three prize winners affiliated to that university. In October of that year, white smoke appeared in the sky over Stockholm and three new popes of economics were appointed: Eugene Fama, Lars Peter Hansen and Robert Schiller. This was to reward them for their "empirical analyses on asset prices". Good enough in itself, but unfortunately the members of the jury did not take the time to explain whether these analyses were pertinent vis-à-vis financial imbalances and persistent casual labour and job insecurity. Eugene Fama is associated with the theory of market efficiency according to which financial markets could not be wrong, contrary to those who think it is possible to anticipate or outperform them, i.e. to regularly generate a return higher than that of a market index such as the S&P 500 in New York or the FTSE 100 in London. These markets would be the natural reference for the economy, its perfect and unfathomable God, its alpha and its omega. The very existence of a crisis contradicts this theory. If financial markets are always right, why do they so suddenly change their opinion, as is the case during a market crash when no new piece of information justifies such a change? The official statement is rather perplexing: the laureate demonstrated that it is extremely difficult to predict stock prices in the short term. This commonplace assertion certainly deserves a Nobel prize… Robert Schiller showed that it was less difficult to foresee long-term stock prices than those in the short term. It is certainly reassuring but, given the unpredictability of short-term forecasts, it could hardly be possible to do worse on the long term. However, as no one is able to define exactly what long term is (1, 3, 5 years?), this result is of no apparent use. The works of these two prize winners are more contradictory than complementary. The former is based on the hypothesis of the rationality of economic agents, whereas the latter analyses their irrational behaviour. Finally, at a time when financial markets rely heavily on central banks and when asset prices are manipulated on a regular basis, it is paradoxical that the

---

[10]It concerned: *Long-Term Capital Management*, with long-term capital only in name on account of the fact that they were short-term bets based on the record indebtedness of this fund.

authors of works on the limited predictability of stock prices are at this point in time given praise and their studies are drawing so much attention! Discussing the sex of angels, it appears, is deserving of the highest reward!

The questions that the Nobel prizes should answer remain in suspense. What are the new economic paradigms that should be developed and what are the solutions that would help put an end to casino finance and get the economy to serve society? Clearly, these questions were not considered pertinent by the members of the jury.

In his will, Alfred Nobel explains that his aim is to reward those who in the preceding year provided the greatest benefits to mankind by way of a prize. That is exactly the objective the jury members should have in mind when they proceed to choose the prize winners. How, for example, did the recipients of the 1997 prize, Robert Merton and Myron Scholes, provide the greatest benefits to mankind by associating themselves with the LTCM fund?

Complacent elites appear at the lower levels of the pyramid of fame. For example, it is interesting to note the case of Frederic Mishkin, professor at Columbia Business School and who, according to the *Monde Diplomatique*,[11] before the outbreak of the crisis, attached his name to a 2006 report entitled "Financial stability in Iceland" for which he received $135,000. According to the same source, professor Richard Portes of the London Business School received £58,000 for a similar expert report.[12]

Economy and finance cannot be solely technical matters to the point of being reserved for the initiated few, a fortiori if they do not play their role. Citizens must take things into their own hands because at the end of the day we are the ones paying for the crisis; it is therefore up to us to demand that those who are initiated contribute towards the solution and not the creation of problems. What we really need to focus on is indignation and engagement to use the terms of Stéphane Hessel.[13]

---

[11]Sigurgeirsdottir, Silla, and Wade, Robert, Quand le peuple islandais vote contre les banquiers, *Le Monde Diplomatique*, May 2011, pp. 1, 18–19.

[12]Portes, Richard, *The Internationalisation of Iceland's Financial Sector* (with Fridrik Mar Baldursson and Frosti Olafsson), Iceland Chamber of Commerce, November 2007, pp. v, 69.

[13]Hessel, Stéphane, *Time for Outrage: Indignez-vous!* Hachette Book Group, USA, 2010.

The spread of "counterfeit intellectual money", i.e. concepts of no value from elites who are very often subservient, contributes towards the failure of the system and the casualisation of the standard of living.

The Political World and Corruption

The political world is to a great extent part of this failure. Today, it is very often a question of pure and simple corruption of the elites. The Greek political class, right and left together, is a perfect example of this.

In this country, it seems more natural to put heavy burdens on European taxpayers, Greek or not, and decrease public servants' pensions and salaries than to require from who receive more undue benefits to pay their taxes.

It was to no avail that when in 2010, Christine Lagarde, then French finance minister, sent her Greek counterpart, George Papaconstantinou, a CD-Rom containing a list of 2063 Greeks who in 2007 had accounts in the Swiss branch of HSBC. However, instead of conducting a painful policy of austerity that only worsened the problems, Greek governments that successively came to power should have guaranteed that taxpayers with accounts abroad paid their taxes. Losses are however enormous. Every year tax fraud costs Greece billions of euros. Up to the moment when the Syriza party won the elections and formed a new government, neither the "socialist" M. Papaconstantinou nor his successors, Evángelos Venizélos who subsequently became the secretary general of his party, and Yannis Stournaras, finance minister up to June 2014, considered it appropriate to use this list to demand that the persons on it pay their taxes. Mr. Papaconstantinou even gave the excuse that this precious CD-Rom had been lost. In his capacity as minister of the economy, he most certainly regretted not having been able to require from some of his friends and colleagues and even certain members of his family to pay their dues! According to the Greek magazine Hot Doc, which published this list in 2012, and the front page of the Wall Street Journal dated 2 November 2012, this list included the names of two former ministers, an advisor to the prime minister elected in 2012,

Mr. Samaras, and well-known Greek businessmen. The Greek journalist responsible for this publication felt the anger of his country's judicial powers for having dared to break the code of silence!

On Friday 28 December 2012, this affair took a new turn when Mr. Papaconstantinou, the former Greek finance minister who received the list, was accused of falsifying it. According to the media, he had deleted the names of two of his cousins, daughters of another ex-minister (a conservative now deceased) and their husbands. Pasok, the party led by his successor Evángelos Venizélos, then announced his expulsion... What will happen to this list? Will the Prime Minister Tsipras' government finally decide to do something about it? According to the former President of the Greek Parliament Zoé Konstantopoulou, it does not appear to be a priority in the eyes of the IMF.

Generally speaking, in numerous countries, the political system is out of breath. The French situation illustrates this well. The major parties, left or right, the "Socialist" Party and the "Republicans" are at a stage of advanced decomposition, plagued as they are by repeated scandals, betrayals and denials of all types. The show they are performing is deplorable and undignified of a so-called democracy. It allows for individuals with no convictions, who are mediocre and corrupt, to be placed in the centre of power.

The current crisis goes beyond a strictly financial setting. It is also a crisis of society's values. With its implicit or explicit justification of the present functioning of the economy, the elite too often plays the role of counterfeiters of thought.[14] Citizens can no longer blindly delegate responsibilities to either technocrats or any political elites. This corruption, this subservience are the evils that must be dealt with very seriously unless we are satisfied with a situation where "we [will] have no conscience left, except, so to speak, the conscience of public opinion and of the criminal code",[15] as Leo Tolstoy wrote in *The Kreutzer Sonata*.

---

[14]See: *L'économie financiarisée et ses faux-monnayeurs*, author Chesney, Marc, *La Littérature face à l'hégémonie de l'économique*, edited by Ursula Bähler and Patrick Labarthe, *Versants*, 58, 2011, pp. 67–77.

[15]Tolstoy, Leo, *The Kreutzer Sonata and Other Stories*, Oxford University Press, USA, 1997.

Bibliography

Benda, Julien, *The Treason of the Intellectuals*, Taylor and Francis, USA, 2007.

Cendrars, Blaise, *La Main coupée* (*1946*), Gallimard, Folio, Paris, 2002.

Chesney, Marc, L'économie financiarisée et ses faux-monnayeurs, in *La Littérature face à l'hégémonie de l'économique*, edited by Ursula Bähler and Patrick Labarthe, Versants, 58, 2011.

Fiodor, Dostoïevski, *A Writer's Diary*, Northwestern Univesity Press, USA, 2009.

Gentile, Emilio, *L'apocalisse della modernità. La Grande Guerra per l'uomo nuovo*, Mondadori, Milan, 2008.

Heinrich, Mann, *Die Verräter, Sämtliche Erzählungen III*, S. Fischer, 1996.

Hessel, Stéphane, *Time for Outrage: Indignez-vous!* Hachette Book Group, USA, 2010.

Nietzsche, Friedrich, *Human, All Too Human*, Cambridge University Press, UK, 1986.

Nietzsche, Friedrich, *Thus Spoke Zarathustra*, Cambridge University Press, USA, 2006.

6

Some Remedies and Solutions

The First World War ended with the disappearance of four empires: the Russian, Austro-Hungarian, Ottoman and German (the Second Reich). Finding solutions for the current crisis requires a profound reconfiguration of empires of another nature and there are at least four: the financial empire of course, along with the energy, military and IT empires which also deserve mention although they are not the subject of this book. By way of the power of their lobbies, they all have a strong hold on our society and cause it to run considerable risks.

The issue of the financial empire has been addressed in the previous chapters. According to the journalist François Fejtö, the reason the First World War became so widespread is linked to "the conviction that a major power can only be maintained by way of expansion[1]". The causes of the prolongation of the crisis are also connected to this phenomenon. It is structured around mega-banks that continue to grow by purchasing other institutions. Waves of deregulation have allowed them to make considerable inroads into and possibly control, even if only partially, sectors such as insurance, energy, metal, foodstuffs, and to force their

---

[1] Fejtö, François, Requiem pour un empire défunt, Paris, Lieu Commun, 1988, p. 30.

© The Author(s) 2018
M. Chesney, *A Permanent Crisis*,
https://doi.org/10.1007/978-3-030-00518-4_6

91

logic on them. In this way, they extend their power with no international regulation envisaging the end of these practices.

The *energy empire* leads the world together with the financial sector. The "gold-dollar standard" has in fact been replaced by the oil-dollar standard with an oil price determined in dollars and a world economy which is shaken by each of its shocks.

The "war against terrorism" being waged in particular in Syria, Iraq and Libya is often the pretext to lay hands on this energy resource.

"Black gold" along with coal generated an increase in CO2 emissions—of close to 40% between 1990 and 2010—which has resulted in considerable risks in terms of global warming for current and future generations.

Shale gas as well as nuclear energy, another component of this empire, also jeopardises populations with unmanageable and uninsurable risks. They also illustrate the domination of the short-term financial logic.

The *military empire* is oversized. It is another indicator of the destructiveness of current power structures. The twentieth century saw the planet bloodstained with wars and deadly conflicts. A century after the onset of the First World War, the situation in Syria and Ukraine threatens to become a dangerous world military conflict. This empire absorbs far too many investments and energy that should be used elsewhere.

The *IT empire* has become the modern control tool of populations, allowing States, "democratic" or not, to intercept national and international communications via Internet, telephone, fax… This empire also contributes to giving democracy a virtual nature. Recent investigations show how European government administration's IT depends on a few dominant providers. As digital systems are growing in size and importance, countries are becoming increasingly dependent on these private corporations.

Reconfiguring these empires, radically changing the way society works in order to find solutions to today's profound crises, would presuppose that politicians really address the problems and assume their responsibilities to serve their constituents and citizens in general. Lloyd George, appointed British Prime Minister in December 1916, remarked with regard to the origins of the war and the attitude of the French head of State and Russian foreign minister, "One feels that Poincaré and

Sazonov have said to each other: what matters is not to prevent war but to look as if we have done everything to do so".[2] Today, citizens also feel that many politicians are trying to give the impression of wanting to solve the serious challenges our society is faced with instead of actually doing it.

This book focuses on the financial empire, on the disquieting power leading society down an uncontrolled spiral, at a turning point characterised as follows:

- Financial markets are no longer able to operate. On the contrary, as the present situation shows, they generate a considerable systemic risk and contribute to the development of casino finance.
- Banks, alleged to be "too big to fail", are subsidised. They are encouraged to engage in risky activities at the expense of taxpayers, shareholders, clients, employees, i.e. the economy and they behave like pyromaniac firefighters.
- The financial sector enslaves the economy and stifles society.
- The invisible hand of Adam Smith has become the myth of this perverted religion which is casino finance. It is less and less effective to the extent that for major banks and investment funds, meeting their specific interests increasingly harms the common good and the economy.
- Economic growth is no longer able to promote true social development. It cannot cure the cancer from which society is suffering. It is supposed to allow for the reimbursement of huge accumulated debt. It is a utopia. Conversely, debt does not engender sustainable growth.
- The direct consequence of the financial grip on the economy is the fraying of democracy the basic principles of which are violated.

The problems described in this book and summed up in these six characteristics have solutions, which more often than not are just a question of common sense. However, they are not implemented. The measures

---

[2]Ibid., pp. 35 and 36 or the special issue of the satirical magazine Crapouillot on World War One, 1935.

taken by governments until now have a different orientation and, at the end of the day, have proven to be ineffective. They are a bitter pill that does not correspond to what is at stake. The answers are not to be found in central banks' low interest rate monetary policies, nor in the tax policy conducted by numerous governments, characterised by increasing austerity. Globally speaking, both debts and risks are too high for traditional tax and monetary policies to be effective.

Why has the course been kept when these policies have led society to a deadlock? Powerful lobbies are at work to prevent the needed paradigm shift beyond the financial and monetary dominance that has ruled nearly all relevant areas of society and economy until now. They are able to almost empty reform projects of their content, such as in the case of taxing financial transactions in Europe, where veritable non-reforms are presented with much publicity! These lobbies work behind the scenes so that governments, that should represent the interests of their voters, and central banks, allegedly independent of political power, are in fact under the influence of the financial sector. Lobbies are behind a grand scale manipulation of public opinion. The basic ingredient is the fear of upsetting financial markets. Generating it allows authorities to implement policies that meet the interests of an ultra-minority caste but which are dangerous for the common mortal.

The absence of the application of true measures means the crisis has an almost permanent nature. Since its onset, very little has been accomplished despite the number of meetings organised at the highest level and their media coverage arrangements. Contrary to what many bankers and regulators state, the resilience of the system has not really been strengthened.

This almost permanent nature is the result of a pseudo-democracy where a number of politicians lose sight of their duty to work for the common good, as they are too busy defending their interests and those of powerful finance lobbies. Solving this crisis, curing this cancer that is eating away at society, essentially requires respect for basic principles: on the one hand reviving democracy, bringing it out of its coma, and on the other hand getting the economy to serve society. In order to meet this second principle, it is essential to remedy the growing complexity of the financial sector. This requires simple and transparent measures that should fit onto a limited number of pages. The new regulations are too complex and too long. For example, Basel III regulations consist of a document of close to 600 pages which are very difficult to implement, whereas the preceding Basel I and II standards had approximately 30 and 300 pages, respectively. This inflationary trend is counterproductive as only major banks have the necessary resources to process and implement these measures. The smaller banks have the greatest difficulty in adjusting and tend to seek integration into a large group. Big banks thus become bigger.

Executing these simple principles requires the application of serious measures adapted to the problems. We shall propose a number of them. Given the gravity of the current situation described in this book, certain readers may think that it is only a question of palliative care, and that these measures do not have the potential to truly cure society. Well, by focusing on democracy, as well as the financial sector, central to the expansion of the casino economy, they can result in the required impact.

Other readers will be of the opinion that they are not realistic. Their implementation will indeed be difficult but attacking the core of the issue will result in the cure of a number of current ills.

Measures to Revive Democracy

– Establishing a true direct democracy, so that citizens may propose that controversial topics be discussed and be finally bound by means of a referendum. In countries such as France, Germany, the UK or Italy, the number of signatures required to launch this type of referendum should be no more than one million. It is inconceivable that in so-called democratic countries, essential issues—be they of a political, energy, social, economic or financial nature—are not addressed democratically and that at the end of the day they are the result of an arbitrary decision taken by the government. The fact that a monarch is elected does not diminish his capacity as monarch, and this even more so if on the one hand, once elected he forgets his election programme and on the other, he takes arbitrary decisions pressurised by powerful lobbies. In France, for example, the monarch elected[3] every 5 years has a palace, the Elysée, an allocated annual budget of 100 million euros and an excessive staff: around 800 people work for him: chefs, chauffeurs, a regular full-time hairdresser without mentioning press officers and all types of sycophants. When he travels around the country, around 1000 members of the police force are usually mobilised for his safety!

The establishment of such a direct democracy would probably mean the creation of an international network of citizens who would unite around a number of basic principles. Serious economic, social and environmental problems, with which we are confronted, require global solutions. Finding these solutions and endeavouring to implement them, as well as generally trying to revive democracy, should be the aim of such a network. It should operate without professional politicians paid by militants or public funds. Indeed, on the one hand, these politicians are cut off from the real world to which they are supposed to devote themselves, and on the other hand, such payments could lead to corruption and misappropriation of all sorts. A network of citizens that works without professional politicians allows for more transparency and thus would avoid a system of paid membership and therefore misappropriation of funds, inherent in this system, as can be seen in a number of countries, such as the USA, England or France. A system of nonrecurring collective funding, implemented locally and directly by the members of this network, would allow it to finance its activities: Internet sites, information meetings, campaigns…

- Ensure that the fight against terrorism is no longer a pretext to place all citizens under permanent control, which is now the case in the USA and in France in particular after the 11 September 2001 attacks in New York and those in Paris in January and November 2015.

---

[3]General De Gaulle wanted, in his own words, "to put right one hundred and fifty-nine years of History", i.e. to place a kind of king at the head of France, and make up for the death of Louis XVI in 1793.

Citizens are entitled to respect for their private sphere. A democracy should not tolerate telephone calls being continually tapped and people's emails being read. A democratic control of the institutions carrying out this large-scale surveillance should be established.
— Guarantee that freedom of press is not merely theoretical but that it is carried out in practice. In particular, digital media that, in order to remain independent, exclude all financing from advertising, should not be stifled by a scandalously high VAT rate.

Measures Concerning the Financial Sector

Financial Sector Regulation

— Bank indebtedness should be strictly limited. Capital requirements are too lax. For large banks, equity currently corresponds in the best-case scenario to close to 4 or 5% of total assets. It should represent at least 20 or 30%, as was very often the case in the nineteenth and early twentieth century.[4]

When a family borrows money to buy a house, a capital contribution of 4% is insufficient. A minimum of 20% of the value of the property is generally required. Why should large banks, for their own affairs, exempt themselves from the constraints they impose on their clients?

They have succeeded, thanks to intense lobbying, to weaken the initial versions of what are known as the Basel III accords,[5] one of the objectives being precisely to marginally limit their huge debt. It is the same institutions that voice their complaints, by alleging that developed countries have colossal debts which have precisely increased due to their bailout starting in 2008.

---

[4]The following book is an interesting reference as regards banks' equity: Admati, Anat and Hellwig, Martin, *The Bankers' New Clothes*, Princeton University Press, USA, 2013.

[5]Basel III Accords: the Basel III accords, published by the Basel committee (hosted by the Bank for International Settlements) in December 2010 and revised in June 2011, seek to regulate the banking sector in order to stabilise the financial system. These attempts, however, remain timid and under the control of financial lobbies.

Furthermore, limiting major banks indebtedness will only generate a truly stabilising effect if this measure is accompanied by a substantial reduction in their off-balance sheet activities, which can only be accomplished by drastically limiting the volume of derivative deals.

In order to more realistically assess these banks' risk, their total commitments including not only those appearing on the balance sheet but also those on the opaque off-balance sheet should be considered. Special purpose vehicles, for example, are ad hoc entities—financial creativity is limitless—that allow major banks to enhance the appearance of their balance sheet by "extracting" their bad assets. Their real risks are therefore camouflaged and their commitments appear less significant than they really are.

Subsequently, if their equity is compared to all their commitments, on- and off-balance sheet, as should be the case, they run the risk of corresponding to much lower percentages than the 4 or 5% officially announced.

- Investment banks should be separated from deposit banks, as was the case in the USA under the Glass–Steagall Act up to 1999. Such a separation protects the clients of deposit banks as it forbids investment banks from gambling with their savings. It would be a stabilising factor.
- The size of banks should be limited. Powerful bank conglomerates are encouraged to take risks without having to assume the consequences. They benefit from free insurance at the taxpayers' expense.
- The astronomical compensation packages of bank CEOs should come to an end. They should be made responsible for dubious deals made at taxpayer expense.
- Within major banks, risk management and control centres should be reconfigured. They should be empowered. It would be more useful to give to employees of these centres bonuses rather than to traders. Today, it is precisely the opposite that is observed, which shows where these banks' priorities lie.
- Hedge fund activities should be strongly regulated and controlled. Generally speaking, the power of the shadow banking system, in

which these funds are included, is particularly worrying. This underground system is bad for the economy.

Certification and Control of Products Issued by Banks

– Before being marketed, financial products should be certified to ensure they meet certain standards, as is the case in other branches of activities. A supervisory authority should be responsible for the eventual certification of these products. The aim is to stop the distribution of toxic financial products and to call it what it is: an offence. Such distribution should be perceived as economically, environmentally and socially harmful.

  – Securitisation activities, defined in Chapter 4, should be strictly supervised, even forbidden. Allowing banks to sell toxic products increases the systemic risk.
  – Over-the-counter financial transactions should be regulated. They also create an additional systemic risk. Financial products, known as derivatives, should be transparently traded, either on organised or on OTC markets, and should mainly meet hedging needs. The distribution of financial products, which permit betting on the default of companies or countries, such as Credit Default Swaps, would therefore be tightly limited.

Taxes and Taxation of Financial Transactions

– The hypocrisy of tax evasion should be put to an end. It could disappear if OECD countries really wanted it to.

The USA, for example, has allowed the State of Delaware to become a tax haven, where creating a fictitious company is child's play. If OECD countries forbid all transactions into and out of tax havens, the problem would essentially be solved. Putting an end to hypocrisy in this area also implies guaranteeing that European political leaders, and in particular the President of the European Commission, supposedly fighting against tax evasion are not those who promoted and organised it to their own benefit and at the expense of many European countries. The "LuxLeaks" revelations in November and December 2014 brought to light secret tax agreements from 2002 until 2010 between over 300 multinational companies and the tax services of Luxembourg that allowed these companies—such as Pepsi, IKEA, FedEx, Walt Disney, Skype, Bombardier and Koch Industries as well as other companies a dozen of which were Greek—to largely escape paying taxes in their countries of origin. These illicit activities were carried out thanks to the creation of so-called letterbox companies, i.e. companies with no real activities in Luxembourg and that use complex and opaque accounting and tax schemes set up by top auditing firms, such as PricewaterhouseCoopers, Ernst & Young, Deloitte and KPMG; the latter provide consulting services to a number of governments all over the world on their tax laws and the content of their economic policy![6] Who is kidding who?

These schemes were set up with the agreement of the highest authorities of that country. How could Jean-Claude Juncker, who was Finance Minister then Prime Minister of Luxembourg and great defender of the "Luxembourg model", have been elected President of the European Commission in 2014? This same Commission lectures Greece and orders it to reduce its deficit, while its president ran a country that allowed companies active in this country to avoid paying taxes at the expense of the Hellenic Republic.[7] This is becoming farcical! In addition, he refused to establish a public record of shadow or letterbox companies which allows for tax evasion without mentioning money laundering.[8]

---

[6]See: "LuxLeaks 2: le parlement européen prêt à enquêter, mais pas trop", Ludovic Lamant and Dan Israel, Mediapart, 10 December 2014.

[7]Likewise, the Dutch Jeroen Dijsselbloem, former President of Eurogroup and former finance Minister of a country which allows, thanks to a lax tax legislation, companies, such as the Canadian Eldorado, to evade taxation in the country in which it was located: namely Greece. The losses would be at least €1.7 million. See: Comment la Grèce voit ses impôts s'évaporer via l'Europe, Dan Israel, Mediapart, 31 March 2014.

[8]See: Juncker refuse de rendre publiques les données sur les sociétés-écrans, Dan Israel, Mediapart, 12 December 2014.

The tax losses linked to these frauds are enormous and fines are rare. In 2005, KPMG was, however, convicted by the American justice system to pay $456 million for questionable schemes which resulted in tax losses of $2.5 billion for the American Treasury. Likewise, in 2013, Ernst & Young had to pay out an amount of $123 million. The tax optimisation set up by this consultancy firm allowed a number of its clients to unduly reduce their taxes by a total of over two billion dollars.

In France, according to an investigation presented by the television channel France 2 on 9 December 2014, a company such as EDF, 84% of which is held by the French State, also "optimised" its taxes, thanks to the use of branches in Luxembourg and in Ireland and to its participation in a company located in Bermuda![9] The French tax authorities thus lost several billion euros in taxes every year.

– The tax burden is far too high for most households and SMEs. It is poorly distributed and expresses a dysfunction of the State. In a time of digitalisation, taxing so much labour is counterproductive.

The tax system is out of date, unfair and of an exaggerated complexity. The US' tax code illustrates this Kafkaesque drift: it consists of 75,000 pages![10] The financial sector has seized power. This marks the failure of democracy. Its dynamic forces are contrary to social and economic development. It imposes costs and growing complexity on society. The tax system should once again undergo an in-depth revision. For this, one thing is decisive: the volume of electronic transactions is excessively high, in most countries. In Switzerland and in a number of other developed countries, it is approximately 160 and 100 times respective GDPs.

---

[9]See the article entitled: Optimisation fiscale: EDF indirectement mis en garde par le gouvernement, Le Monde.fr, 10 September 2014.

[10]In 1913, it only had 400 pages. This complexity generates huge costs for the American taxpayer; 6.1 billion hours each year is spent trying to understand the pertinent passages of this code and to complete the tax return, which corresponds to a total cost of close to $234 billion. Cf. Federal Tax Laws and Regulations Are Now Over 10 Million Words Long, Scott Greenberg, 8 October 2015, Tax Foundation.

A tax on all electronic payments should be introduced.[11] A rate of 0.2% or even 0.5% or 1% would be low in comparison with the VAT rate, but certainly already too high for the financial lobbies. In view of the financial amounts in circulation, it would represent a true manna for most of the States currently over-indebted.

Switzerland offers a particularly interesting example of the flows such a tax would create. Electronic transactions reach an enormous amount of at least CHF 100,000 billion francs![12] A tax of only 0.2% on every electronic transfer would bring in CHF200 billion francs, i.e. a little below a third of the Swiss GDP. This amount is higher than the sum of all the taxes collected in this country, estimated at around CHF140 billion. In short, a low automatic tax on all electronic payments would theoretically allow this country, and most others, to reduce, maybe even abolish, most other taxes! Theoretically of course, as this would result in a reduction in the number of transactions on stock markets, bond markets, Forex markets …, it would probably be necessary to increase it to 0.5 or 1% for it to keep its profitable nature. A reduction in the volume of financial transactions would, however, be very useful as it would also help decrease the unbridled speculation on financial markets. Such

---

[11]As far as I know, this idea was initially introduced in the 1970s by René Montgranier, who presented it as "the egg of Columbus". See his book entitled: *La Clé de la crise*, Éditions économiques financières et sociales, 1985, pp. 108–120, as well as the article: Pour une taxe sur tous les mouvements de fonds, Multitudes 3/2011. In the 1990s, Professor Edgar Feige, from the University of Wisconsin, then subsequently Simon Thorpe, director of research at CNRS at Toulouse, as well as Bernard Dupont in Genève, developed a similar idea. Felix Bolliger, in his article "Reinvent the System – Microsteuer auf Gesamtzahlungsverkehr", 2013, also worked on this concept.

[12]See annexe 2 of the monthly bulletin of economic statistics of the National Swiss Bank (BNS) of April 2013 "Trafic des paiements dans le Swiss Interbank Clearing SIC", cited by Bolliger, Felix. The calculation method used by BNS was altered between January and April 2013, and payment traffic for 2012 therefore dropped from close to CHF95,000 billion to approximately CHF30,000 billion (and reached CHF43,000 billion in 2017). Transfers between the current accounts of banks to BNS and their financial trading accounts in the SIC system are from then on excluded from the data. Despite this statistical reduction, financial transfers continue to be extremely high because the SIC system only records a part of the transactions. One has to consider those that on foreign exchange markets (FOREX) concern the franc that add an amount of close to CHF50,000 billion a year, treated either over-the-counter or on the EBS platform. One also has to consider transfers made inside each financial establishment, operations on derivatives and check that the high-frequency transactions have been taken into account... An estimate of CHF100,000 billion for the total number of transactions appears to be fairly conservative.

a tax would also have the advantage of seriously limiting tax fraud as all electronic transfers are in principle automatically detected and recorded. This issue should soon be addressed in Switzerland with the launch of a so-called popular initiative.

In the case of France and Germany, as in most developed countries, with a conservative estimate of all electronic financial transactions corresponding to 100 times GDP, a rate of 0.25% would suffice to generate an amount greatly exceeding all current tax revenues.[13]

Therefore, a single and simple micro-tax with particularly low costs of collection should be, on the international level, supported by States and by households and most companies as it would mean simplification of administrative work and a large drop in taxes. Yet, it has not even been considered! Why? It obviously fails to please major banks responsible for the overwhelming majority of financial transactions. With such a tax, big banks and most hedge funds would pay more taxes than is currently the case, and tax optimisation and tricks of all types would be more difficult to apply!

Such a tax would also help reduce market volatility and would have another positive effect of almost putting an end to financial transactions conducted in milli- or microseconds.

It should be noted that such a tax, even introduced in a limited number of countries, would already have positive effects. On the one hand, it would stabilise the economy of those countries as casino finance activities would tend to be moved abroad. On the other hand, it would have a knock-on effect on citizens and companies of other countries who would look on with interest and see that it is possible to really reduce taxes and simplify the fiscal system.

Mention should be made that this tax idea differs from the famous Tobin tax. Indeed, it should not be added to already existing ones but would tend to replace them, by reducing the tax burden of most households and companies, especially SMEs, and by increasing that of big

---

[13]See: Un économiste veut remplacer tous les impôts par une seule taxe, Julien Marion, BFM, 30 October 2016.

banks which are undertaxed.[14] Furthermore, it is not a question of only taxing financial transactions on stocks, bonds or foreign exchange but rather on all electronic payments, including, for example, those concerning supermarket or restaurant invoices and cash machines.

In 2012, 11 European countries decided to move towards the "Tobin tax", and eventually and experimentally, one can never be too careful to create a tax on financial transactions "TFT". This project, much less ambitious than that of the European Commission in 2011, should have generated over €30 billion a year. Today, there are still numerous doubts about the implementation of this project. At the time this book is being written, what is certain is that if this is created, it will be under the form of a version with no real reach, contrary to the commitments of the heads of state and government of these 11 countries. Here too, powerful lobbies are clearly at work. At the end of 2014, the French Minister of the Economy, Michel Sapin, did not envisage more than one tax limited to stocks and excluding most derivatives. The rate currently in force in France is 0.2% in comparison with 0.5% in the UK.[15] It is perceived for share transactions of French companies whose stock capitalisation is over €1 billion. It should be changed to 0.3% if the decision taken by MPs on 20 October 2016 in Paris[16] is not amended. Financial lobbies are nevertheless at work for parliamentarians to change their minds. Derivatives are not affected by this tax, and they are not expected to be either. What a felicitous gift for large French banks, such as BNP Paribas, Société Générale or Crédit-Agricole, very active in these products! Therefore, the profits on these activities will not be reduced, and in case of losses, the taxpayer will be called to the rescue! Are we talking about that entrepreneurial spirit so highly commended by those French governments that come to power, or the nth episode of a grotesque farce? The reader will have understood that the author of this book thinks it is the latter!

---

[14]To this regard, see the statements made by Gerry Rice, IMF spokesperson in Washington, on 31 January 2013. According to Rice, "The financial sector is undertaxed and must pay an equitable part in order to attenuate the costs of the current crisis…".

[15]Stamp duty.

[16]The extension of this tax to intra-day trading was also planned.

If the change to 0.3% is confirmed, this tax will generate between 2 and 4 billion euros compared with the approximately 545 billion euros that the micro-tax presented above would generate at a rate of 0.25%[17] on all electronic transactions. That is to say that the current projects, presented as ambitious and with a view to forcing the financial sector to contribute towards the resolution of the problems that it itself created, are essentially inapt. Only crumbs from the table are recovered at the expense of society.

The book by Christian Chavagneux and Thierry Philipponnat[18] describes the links that unite the worlds of politics and finance. According to them: "*In France, capture is basically sociological due to the organised system of revolving doors and the well-known inbreeding of the financial elites. This situation, combined with the extreme concentration of the French banking system, explains the unconfessed but very real will of Paris not to reform the structure of the banks*".

This porosity between political sectors and financial lobbies was once again recently illustrated in November 2014 by way of the transfer[19] of the head of "financial and monetary affairs" of the permanent representation of France to the European Institutions, Benoît de La Chapelle, to the French Banking Federation (FBF), where he now holds the position of director delegated to this lobby of the French banking industry. While the negotiations in Brussels concerning the introduction of a tax on financial transactions were still at a deadlock, one of the spokespersons and French specialists on the subject, supposed to defend this tax project, joined a lobby ferociously opposed to the introduction of such a tax. The reader will judge whether this is capture or corruption of the elites, or both at the same time!

---

[17]This means a quarter of the French GDP which in 2015 represented €2.181 billion.

[18]La Capture, La Découverte, 2014.

[19]See the article: Taxe Tobin: les banques font leur marché chez les hauts fonctionnaires, Ludovic Lamant, Mediapart, 9 December 2014.

Debt Auditing and Control of Rating Agencies

The indebtedness of numerous States is disproportionate. Defaults are to be expected. An audit of the debt[20] of certain countries, such as Greece, would be desirable, in particular as the partial cancellation of the Greek debt continues to be refused by its creditors. The March 2015 creation of the initiative of the Truth Committee on Public Debt, by the ex-President of the Greek Parliament Ms. Konstantopoulou, was a first step in this direction. "*The aim is to determine the eventual odious, illegal or illegitimate nature of the public debts contracted by the Greek government*", she indicated. Article 7 of the regulation adopted in May 2013 by the European Union (EU) in fact sets out that "*a member State being the object of a macroeconomic adjustment programme shall perform a full audit of its public finances in order to assess the reasons that led to the accumulation of excessive debts and to detect any eventual irregularities*".

Such an idea had been implemented in the past in Ecuador by the former President of the Republic, Rafael Correa. The aim, among others, is to determine whether public contracts having led to an increase in debt had been tainted by corruption or not. Analysing the origin of debts helps identify those that will be reimbursed and those that should not.

Both Greece's debts towards Germany and Germany's towards Greece should be taken into consideration and serious talks between the two governments should help clarify the situation. During the Second World War and the occupation of Greece by German troops, this country suffered greatly. As the former resistance fighter, Manolis Glezos, wrote in his book,[21] 13.5% of the population perished at the time,[22] of which 600,000 died of hunger and 105,000 were deported to concentration camps never to return. Vast infrastructure including roads and railways was destroyed during the occupation. The sums at stake are impressive. They are associated with pillaged archaeological treasures,

---

[20]See the publications on this topic of the Committee for the Abolition of Illegitimate Debt (CADTM).

[21]Even if it were a single Deutsche Mark, published by Livanis publishers in Athens in 2012.

[22]The Jewish community of Thessaloniki was almost totally exterminated by the Nazis: close to 54,000 people from a total of 56,000 were killed.

having been occupied by the Nazis in 1941 (currently around €54 billion without interest), war reparations and compensation for the families of victims.

– Rating agencies must be controlled. They have exorbitant power that has a negative effect on the smooth running of the economy. The objective would be to make their leaders accountable for the ratings issued by their agencies so they may be legally required to account for their actions in the case of a financial crash or defaults accentuated by their ratings. The financial crisis has shown the risk these agencies represent. They have assigned the best ratings to the most dubious financial products. If they had worked more objectively, they would probably have lost their contracts with the banks involved that pay them directly. Since 2010, they have tried to improve their image by being particularly strict with a number of countries, e.g. Greece. Running with the pack is so tempting.

Rethinking the Teaching of Economics and Finance

The programmes and contents of economics and finance courses should be treated with great care, as called on by way of the appeal of researchers and teachers launched in 2011 and referred to in the preceding chapter. Too often, when reading course outlines, the question is raised whether the crisis really started in 2007–2008! Analysing the damage that it caused and drawing lessons from the consequences are therefore essential. Yet, that does not appear to be an academic priority! Every year hordes of young graduates leave the educational system with a master's in economics, in Finance or an MBA, without their education having instilled in them the necessary critical spirit. They have been trained to apply the financial logic and at the end of the day casino finance to the detriment of all others: that of society, that of the economy, that of specific sectors of activity, even that of the company in which they will works.

Conclusion

Finally, the implementation of all these measures requires citizens and politicians to be able to analyse the situation and to demonstrate the will to find real solutions as well as a lot of courage. The author is aware that doing so will not be an easy task, neither now nor in the future, and will require time. Paradoxically, it is more than a priority to get the economy and society out of the deadlock it is in. Finally, it is a choice of society, a choice between the dictatorship of the financial sector and a democracy where active citizens take their future in their own hands. We have a responsibility vis-à-vis present and future generations who have the inalienable right to live in a decent and dignified manner in an accountable and civilised society.

Bibliography

Admati, Anat, and Hellwig, Martin, *The Bankers' New Clothes*, Princeton University Press, USA, 2013.

Chavagneux, Christian, and Philipponnat, Thierry, La Capture, La Découverte, 2014.

Fejtő, François, *Requiem pour un empire défunt*, Lieu Commun, Paris, 1988.

Glezos, Manolis, *Even If It Were a Single Deutsche Mark*, Livanis publishers, Athens, 2012.

Greenberg, Scott, *Federal Tax Laws and Regulations Are Now Over 10 Million Words Long*, Tax Foundation, 8 October 2015.

Montgranier, René, *La Clé de la crise*, Éditions économiques financières et sociales, 1985.

Monthly Bulletin of Economic Statistics of the National Swiss Bank (BNS), "Trafic des paiements dans le Swiss Interbank Clearing SIC", April 2013.

Tolstoy, Leo, *The Kreutzer Sonata and Other Stories*, Oxford University Press, USA, 1997.

Index